AF270267

FALLING IN LOVE

More in the Classic Wisdom for Modern Minds series from Macmillan Collector's Library

Finding Happiness

Leaving Home

Living Peacefully

FALLING IN LOVE

Selection and introduction by Zachary Seager

MACMILLAN COLLECTOR'S LIBRARY

This collection first published 2025 by Macmillan Collector's Library
an imprint of Pan Macmillan
The Smithson, 6 Briset Street, London EC1M 5NR
EU representative: Macmillan Publishers Ireland Ltd,
1st Floor, The Liffey Trust Centre, 117–126 Sheriff Street Upper,
Dublin 1, D01 YC43
Associated companies throughout the world
www.panmacmillan.com

ISBN 978-1-0350-4565-5

The Permissions Acknowledgements on p. 157
constitute an extension of this copyright page.

1 3 5 7 9 8 6 4 2

A CIP catalogue record for this book is available from the British Library.

Typeset in Platin by Jouve (UK), Milton Keynes
Printed and bound in China by Imago

Contents

HOW?

Introduction

'Love is madness.' So says Socrates in Plato's *Phaedrus*, a philosophical dialogue written 2,400 years ago. Despite the intervening millennia, we don't seem to have made much progress on the subject.

Falling in love is an eternal question, a beguiling mystery that by turns enthrals, enrages and electrifies most people on the planet. It has provided material for poems and stories since poetry and storytelling began; subjugated kings, queens and emperors; nourished thought in religion and ethics; and provided twenty-nine seasons and counting of the TV show *The Bachelor*.

Falling in love puzzles and delights in equal measure. We struggle to comprehend other people's relationships: perplexed by the latest passion of a close friend, we shrug and say that love is blind. Meanwhile, our own objects of affection appear self-evidently exceptional. We occasionally find ourselves feeling snobbish like the French aphorist François de la Rochefoucauld ('there are some people who would never fall in love if they hadn't heard love talked about'). And yet we know this to be false: even the most prosaic among us fall at some point for love's poetry. We laugh along with the American writer Ambrose Bierce, who described love as 'temporary insanity curable by marriage'. But we end up marvelling at aged couples wandering hand in hand despite the late hour, still apparently mad with love.

For the celebrated Scottish author Robert Louis Stevenson, 'there is only one event in life which really astonishes a man and startles him out of his prepared opinions' – falling in love. It holds a unique place in our imagination. And it can make even the most eloquent among us feel suddenly lost for words (acclaimed novelist Edith Wharton to her on-again-off-again lover William Morton Fullerton: 'if, when you hold me and I don't speak, it's because all the words in me seem to have become throbbing pulses, and all my thoughts are a great golden blur').

Falling in love escapes even the most brilliant of analysts. Poets and playwrights from Sophocles to Tom Stoppard keep writing about the subject not just to satisfy an endless appetite for such tales, but because there always seems more to say. Socrates himself appeared in awe of love. Its pull is so powerful that even Adam Smith felt compelled to consider the subject, albeit with the ardour to be expected of a man often described as the father of economics ('there is a satisfaction in the consciousness of being loved which [. . .] is of more importance to happiness than all the advantages which [one] can expect to derive from it').

Falling in love is an undying enigma, a mystery so large that some deny its very existence, attributing its strange magic to basic biology. It's true that people fall ill with it every day. But love seems curiously unaffected by such claims. If it is in fact an illusion, we're all still easily fooled by it. And though the whole process of falling in love can feel like a riddle without an answer, this doesn't stop poets and philosophers, novelists and musicians, painters, filmmakers, photographers, journalists, television producers, publishing professionals, academics and adults of all ages – as well as children, teenagers and in many cases household pets – from trying to figure out just what on earth is going on.

This anthology presents the efforts of some

of the greatest minds in history as they seek to answer fundamental questions about falling in love. What is it? How does it seize us and overwhelm us? Why does it happen at all? And if love is so great, why do we often wish to forget about it altogether?

The simplest questions are often the hardest to answer. That's why this book is divided into three sections, with each part centred on a different aspect of falling in love: 'what', 'why' and 'how'. But though the authors in this anthology all address similar questions, they arrive at surprising and surprisingly divergent conclusions.

In one of his dialogues, for instance, Plato forges a myth to explain love, telling us why we all seek our long-lost other halves. American philosopher and sage Ralph Waldo Emerson considers the metaphysics of love. In contrast, the French novelist Stendhal uses his practical experience and earthy wit to penetrate love's secret mechanisms and the many forms it can take. The British Romantic poet Percy Shelley raises love to heavenly heights while the Austrian modernist Rainer Maria Rilke considers the extraordinary demands that love makes of us.

Some authors focus exclusively on the 'why' of love. In an essay befitting one of the pioneers of modern science, the philosopher and statesman Francis Bacon reflects on what the myth of Cupid can tell us about the world. Others like American memoirist Mae M. Franking concentrate on the 'how', describing in moving terms the way she herself fell in love with a young Chinese student in Ann Arbor, Michigan, in 1907. Franking details the prejudice and disapproval she and her partner faced from their respective families and cultures, but the heart of her story is the triumph of their love. Others still – like the Lithuanian-born anarchist Emma Goldman – wonder if love can truly thrive in a world fixated on marriage and property. Only a select few writers like Robert Louis Stevenson rove happily all around the vast field of love's mystery.

The Greek poet Sappho (*c.* 630 BCE–*c.* 570 BCE) closes out the anthology. Long before Socrates, she knew that love was madness – and that this madness seemed at times the very meaning of our lives. And yet, ever the wisest among us, Sappho thinks not of love but of her beloved. Her work shows that love is not just a concept, never just an idea, but also a faith and an act. Along with the other authors in this book, she demonstrates that there are many ways to care for another person, many facets to falling in love.

What?

PERCY BYSSHE SHELLEY

On Love

What is love? Ask him who lives, what is life? ask him who adores, what is God?

I know not the internal constitution of other men, nor even thine, whom I now address. I see that in some external attributes they resemble me, but when, misled by that appearance, I have thought to appeal to something in common, and unburthen my inmost soul to them, I have found my language misunderstood, like one in a distant and savage land. The more opportunities they have afforded me for experience, the wider has appeared the interval between us, and to a greater distance have the points of sympathy been withdrawn. With a spirit ill fitted to sustain such proof, trembling and feeble through its tenderness, I have everywhere sought sympathy, and have found only repulse and disappointment.

Thou demandest what is love? It is that

powerful attraction towards all that we conceive, or fear, or hope beyond ourselves, when we find within our own thoughts the chasm of an insufficient void, and seek to awaken in all things that are, a community with what we experience within ourselves. If we reason, we would be understood; if we imagine, we would that the airy children of our brain were born anew within another's; if we feel, we would that another's nerves should vibrate to our own, that the beams of their eyes should kindle at once and mix and melt into our own, that lips of motionless ice should not reply to lips quivering and burning with the heart's best blood. This is Love. This is the bond and the sanction which connects not only man with man, but with every thing which exists. We are born into the world, and there is something within us which, from the instant that we live, more and more thirsts after its likeness. It is probably in correspondence with this law that the infant drains milk from the bosom of its mother; this propensity develops itself with the development of our nature. We dimly see within our intellectual nature a miniature as it were of our entire self, yet deprived of all that we condemn or despise, the ideal prototype of every thing excellent or lovely that we are capable of conceiving as belonging to the nature of man. Not only the portrait of our external being, but an assemblage of the minutest particles of which our nature is composed; a mirror whose surface reflects only the forms of purity and brightness; a soul within our soul that describes a circle around its proper paradise, which pain, and sorrow, and evil dare not overleap. To this we eagerly refer all sensations, thirsting that they should resemble or correspond with it. The discovery of its antitype; the meeting with an understanding capable of clearly estimating our own; an imagination which should enter into and seize upon the subtle and delicate peculiarities which we have delighted to cherish and unfold in secret; with a frame whose nerves, like the chords of two exquisite lyres, strung to the accompaniment of one delightful voice, vibrate with the vibrations of our own; and of a combination of all these in such proportion as the type within demands; this is the invisible and unattainable point to which Love tends; and to attain which, it urges forth the powers of man to arrest the faintest shadow of that, without the possession of which there is no rest nor respite to the heart over which it rules. Hence in solitude, or in that deserted state when we are surrounded by human beings, and yet they sympathise not with us, we love the flowers, the grass, and the waters, and the sky. In the motion of the very leaves of spring, in the blue air, there is then found a secret correspondence with our heart. There is eloquence in the tongueless wind, and a melody in the flowing brooks and the rustling of the reeds beside them, which by their inconceivable relation to something within the soul, awaken the spirits to a dance of breathless rapture, and bring tears of mysterious tenderness to the eyes, like the enthusiasm of patriotic success, or the voice of one beloved singing to you alone. Sterne says that, if he were in a desert, he would love some cypress. So soon as this want or power is dead, man becomes the living sepulchre of himself, and what yet survives is the mere husk of what once he was.

AMBROSE BIERCE

love, *n.*

love, ***n.*** A temporary insanity curable by marriage or by removal of the patient from the influences under which he incurred the disorder. This disease, like *caries* and many other ailments, is prevalent only among civilized races living under artificial conditions; barbarous nations breathing pure air and eating simple food enjoy immunity from its ravages. It is sometimes fatal, but more frequently to the physician than to the patient.

RALPH WALDO EMERSON

Love

Every promise of the soul has innumerable fulfilments; each of its joys ripens into a new want. Nature, uncontainable, flowing, forelooking, in the first sentiment of kindness anticipates already a benevolence which shall lose all particular regards in its general light. The introduction to this felicity is in a private and tender relation of one to one, which is the enchantment of human life; which, like a certain divine rage and enthusiasm, seizes on man at one period, and works a revolution in his mind and body; unites him to his race, pledges him to the domestic and civic relations, carries him with new sympathy into nature, enhances the power of the senses, opens the imagination, adds to his character heroic and sacred attributes, establishes marriage, and gives permanence to human society.

The natural association of the sentiment

of love with the heyday of the blood seems to require, that in order to portray it in vivid tints, which every youth and maid should confess to be true to their throbbing experience, one must not be too old. The delicious fancies of youth reject the least savour of a mature philosophy, as chilling with age and pedantry their purple bloom. And, therefore, I know I incur the imputation of unnecessary hardness and stoicism from those who compose the Court and Parliament of Love. But from these formidable censors I shall appeal to my seniors. For it is to be considered that this passion of which we speak, though it begin with the young, yet forsakes not the old, or rather suffers no one who is truly its servant to grow old, but makes the aged participators of it, not less than the tender maiden, though in a different and nobler sort. For it is a fire that, kindling its first embers in the narrow nook of a private bosom, caught from a wandering spark out of another private heart, glows and enlarges until it warms and beams upon multitudes of men and women, upon the universal heart of all, and so lights up the whole world and all nature with its generous flames. It matters not, therefore, whether we attempt to describe the passion at twenty, at thirty, or at eighty years. He who paints it at the first period will lose some of its later, he who paints it at the last, some of its earlier traits. Only it is to be hoped that, by patience and the Muses' aid, we may attain to that inward view of the law, which shall describe a truth ever young and beautiful, so central that it shall commend itself to the eye, at whatever angle beholden.

And the first condition is, that we must leave a too close and lingering adherence to facts, and study the sentiment as it appeared in hope and not in history. For each man sees his own life defaced and disfigured, as the life of man is not, to his imagination. Each man sees over his own experience a certain stain of error, whilst that of other men looks fair and ideal. Let any man go back to those delicious relations which make the beauty of his life, which have given him sincerest instruction and nourishment, he will shrink and moan. Alas! I know not why, but infinite compunctions embitter in mature life the remembrances of budding joy, and cover every beloved name. Every thing is beautiful seen from the point of the intellect, or as truth. But all is sour, if seen as experience. Details are melancholy; the plan is seemly and noble. In the actual world—the painful kingdom of time and place—dwell care, and canker, and fear. With thought, with the ideal, is immortal hilarity, the rose of joy. Round it all the Muses sing. But grief cleaves to names, and persons, and the partial interests of today and yesterday.

The strong bent of nature is seen in the proportion which this topic of personal relations usurps in the conversation of society. What do we wish to know of any worthy person so much, as how he has sped in the history of this sentiment? What books in the circulating libraries circulate? How we glow over these novels of passion, when the story is told with any spark of truth and nature! And what fastens attention, in the intercourse of life, like any passage betraying affection between two parties? Perhaps we never saw them before, and never shall meet them again. But we see them exchange a glance, or betray a deep emotion, and we are no longer strangers. We understand them, and take the warmest interest in the development of the romance. All mankind love a lover. The earliest demonstrations of complacency and kindness are nature's most winning pictures. It is the dawn of civility and grace in the coarse and rustic. The rude village boy teases the girls about the school-house door;—but today he comes running into the entry, and meets one fair child disposing her satchel; he holds her books to help her, and instantly it seems to him as if she removed herself from him infinitely, and was a sacred precinct. Among the throng of girls he runs rudely enough, but one alone distances him; and these two little neighbours, that were so close just now, have learned to respect each other's personality. Or who can avert his eyes from the engaging, half-artful, half-artless ways of school-girls who go into the country shops to buy a skein of silk or a sheet of paper, and talk half an hour about nothing with the broad-faced, good-natured shop-boy. In the village they are on a perfect equality, which love delights in, and without any coquetry the happy, affectionate nature of woman flows out in this pretty gossip. The girls may have little beauty, yet plainly do they establish between them and the good boy the most agreeable, confiding relations, what with their fun and their earnest, about Edgar, and Jonas, and Almira, and who was invited to the party, and who danced at the dancing-school, and when the singing-school would begin, and other nothings concerning which the parties cooed. By and by that boy wants a wife, and very truly and heartily will he know where to find a sincere and sweet mate, without any risk such as Milton deplores as incident to scholars and great men.

I have been told, that in some public discourses of mine my reverence for the intellect has made me unjustly cold to the personal relations. But now I almost shrink at the remembrance of such disparaging words. For persons are love's world, and the coldest philosopher cannot recount the debt of the young soul wandering here in nature to the power of love, without being tempted to unsay, as treasonable to nature, aught derogatory to the social instincts. For, though the celestial rapture falling out of heaven seizes only upon those of tender age, and although a beauty overpowering all analysis or comparison, and putting us quite beside ourselves, we can seldom see after thirty years, yet the remembrance of these visions outlasts all other remembrances, and is a wreath of flowers on the oldest brows. But here is a strange fact; it may seem to many men, in revising their experience, that they have no fairer page in their life's book than the delicious memory of some passages wherein affection contrived to give a witchcraft surpassing the deep attraction of its own truth to a parcel of accidental and trivial circumstances. In looking backward, they may find that several things which were not the charm have more reality to this groping memory than the charm itself which embalmed them. But be our experience in particulars what it may, no man ever forgot the visitations of that power to his heart and brain, which created all things new; which was the dawn in him of music, poetry, and art; which made the face of nature radiant with purple light, the morning and the night varied enchantments; when a single tone of one voice could make the heart bound, and the most trivial circumstance associated with one form is put in the amber of memory; when he became all eye when one was present, and all memory when one was gone; when the youth becomes a watcher of windows, and studious of a glove, a veil, a ribbon, or the wheels of a carriage; when no place is too solitary, and none too silent, for him who has richer company and sweeter conversation in his new thoughts, than any old friends, though best and purest, can give him; for the figures, the motions, the words of the beloved object are not like other images written in water, but, as Plutarch said, "enamelled in fire," and make the study of midnight.

> "Thou art not gone being gone, where'er
>   thou art,
> Thou leav'st in him thy watchful eyes, in
>   him thy loving heart."

In the noon and the afternoon of life we still throb at the recollection of days when happiness was not happy enough, but must be drugged with the relish of pain and fear; for he touched the secret of the matter, who said of love,—

> "All other pleasures are not worth its
> pains";

and when the day was not long enough, but the night, too, must be consumed in keen recollections; when the head boiled all night on the pillow with the generous deed it resolved on; when the moonlight was a pleasing fever, and the stars were letters, and the flowers ciphers, and the air was coined into song; when all business seemed an impertinence, and all the men and women running to and fro in the streets, mere pictures.

The passion rebuilds the world for the youth. It makes all things alive and significant. Nature grows conscious. Every bird on the boughs of the tree sings now to his heart and soul. The notes are almost articulate. The clouds have faces as he looks on them. The trees of the forest, the waving grass, and the peeping flowers have grown intelligent; and he almost fears to trust them with the secret which they seem to invite. Yet nature soothes and sympathizes. In the green solitude he finds a dearer home than with men.

"Fountain-heads and pathless groves,
Places which pale passion loves,
Moonlight walks, when all the fowls
Are safely housed, save bats and owls,
A midnight bell, a passing groan,—
These are the sounds we feed upon."

Behold there in the wood the fine madman! He is a palace of sweet sounds and sights; he dilates; he is twice a man; he walks with arms akimbo; he soliloquizes; he accosts the grass and the trees; he feels the blood of the violet, the clover, and the lily in his veins; and he talks with the brook that wets his foot.

The heats that have opened his perceptions of natural beauty have made him love music and verse. It is a fact often observed, that men have written good verses under the inspiration of passion, who cannot write well under any other circumstances.

The like force has the passion over all his nature. It expands the sentiment; it makes the clown gentle, and gives the coward heart. Into the most pitiful and abject it will infuse a heart and courage to defy the world, so only it have the countenance of the beloved object. In giving him to another, it still more gives him to himself. He is a new man, with new perceptions, new and keener purposes, and a religious solemnity of character and aims. He does not longer appertain to his family and society; *he* is somewhat; *he* is a person; *he* is a soul.

And here let us examine a little nearer the nature of that influence which is thus potent over the human youth. Beauty, whose revelation to man we now celebrate, welcome as the sun wherever it pleases to shine, which pleases everybody with it and with themselves, seems sufficient to itself. The lover cannot paint his maiden to his fancy poor and solitary. Like a tree in flower, so much soft, budding, informing loveliness is society for itself, and she teaches his eye why Beauty was pictured with Loves and Graces attending her steps. Her existence makes the world rich. Though she extrudes all other persons from his attention as cheap and unworthy, she indemnifies him by carrying out her own being into somewhat impersonal, large, mundane, so that the maiden stands to him for a representative of all select things and virtues. For that reason, the lover never sees personal resemblances in his mistress to her kindred or to others. His friends find in her a likeness to her mother, or her sisters, or to persons not of her blood. The lover sees no resemblance except to summer evenings and diamond mornings, to rainbows and the song of birds.

The ancients called beauty the flowering of virtue. Who can analyze the nameless charm which glances from one and another face and form? We are touched with emotions of tenderness and complacency, but we cannot find whereat this dainty emotion, this wandering gleam, points. It is destroyed for the imagination by any attempt to refer it to organization. Nor does it point to any relations of friendship or love known and described in society, but, as it seems to me, to a quite other and unattainable sphere, to relations of transcendent delicacy and sweetness, to what roses and violets hint and foreshow. We cannot approach beauty. Its nature is like opaline doves'-neck lustres, hovering and evanescent. Herein it resembles the most excellent things, which all have this rainbow character, defying all attempts at appropriation and use. What else did Jean Paul Richter signify, when he said to music, "Away! away! thou speakest to me of things which in all my endless life I have not found, and shall not find." The same fluency may be observed in every work of the plastie arts. The statue is then beautiful when it begins to be incomprehensible, when it is passing out of criticism, and can no longer be defined by compass and measuring-wand, but demands an active imagination to go with it, and to say what it is in the act of doing. The god or hero of the sculptor is always represented in a transition *from* that which is representable to the senses, *to* that which is not. Then first it ceases to be a stone. The same remark holds of painting. And of poetry, the success is not attained when it lulls and satisfies, but when it astonishes and fires us with new endeavours after the unattainable. Concerning it, Landor inquires "whether it is not to be referred to some purer state of sensation and existence."

In like manner, personal beauty is then first charming and itself, when it dissatisfies us with any end; when it becomes a story without an end; when it suggests gleams and visions, and not earthly satisfactions; when it makes the beholder feel his unworthiness; when he cannot feel his right to it, though he were Cæsar; he cannot feel more right to it than to the firmament and the splendors of a sunset.

Hence arose the saying, "If I love you, what is

that to you?" We say so, because we feel that what we love is not in your will, but above it. It is not you, but your radiance. It is that which you know not in yourself, and can never know.

This agrees well with that high philosophy of Beauty which the ancient writers delighted in; for they said that the soul of man, embodied here on earth, went roaming up and down in quest of that other world of its own, out of which it came into this, but was soon stupefied by the light of the natural sun, and unable to see any other objects than those of this world, which are but shadows of real things. Therefore, the Deity sends the glory of youth before the soul, that it may avail itself of beautiful bodies as aids to its recollection of the celestial good and fair; and the man beholding such a person in the female sex runs to her, and finds the highest joy in contemplating the form, movement, and intelligence of this person, because it suggests to him the presence of that which indeed is within the beauty, and the cause of the beauty.

If, however, from too much conversing with material objects, the soul was gross, and misplaced its satisfaction in the body, it reaped nothing but sorrow; body being unable to fulfil the promise which beauty holds out;

but if, accepting the hint of these visions and suggestions which beauty makes to his mind, the soul passes through the body, and falls to admire strokes of character, and the lovers contemplate one another in their discourses and their actions, then they pass to the true palace of beauty, more and more inflame their love of it, and by this love extinguishing the base affection, as the sun puts out the fire by shining on the hearth, they become pure and hallowed. By conversation with that which is in itself excellent, magnanimous, lowly, and just, the lover comes to a warmer love of these nobilities, and a quicker apprehension of them. Then he passes from loving them in one to loving them in all, and so is the one beautiful soul only the door through which he enters to the society of all true and pure souls. In the particular society of his mate, he attains a clearer sight of any spot, any taint, which her beauty has contracted from this world, and is able to point it out, and this with mutual joy that they are now able, without offence, to indicate blemishes and hindrances in each other, and give to each all help and comfort in curing the same. And, beholding in many souls the traits of the divine beauty, and separating in each soul that which is divine from the taint which it has contracted in the world, the lover ascends to the highest beauty, to the love and knowledge of the Divinity, by steps on this ladder of created souls.

Somewhat like this have the truly wise told us of love in all ages. The doctrine is not old, nor is it new. If Plato, Plutarch, and Apuleius taught it, so have Petrarch, Angelo, and Milton. It awaits a truer unfolding in opposition and rebuke to that subterranean prudence which presides at marriages with words that take hold of the upper world, whilst one eye is prowling in the cellar, so that its gravest discourse has a savor of hams and powdering-tubs. Worst, when this sensualism intrudes into the education of young women, and withers the hope and affection of human nature, by teaching that marriage signifies nothing but a housewife's thrift, and that woman's life has no other aim.

But this dream of love, though beautiful, is only one scene in our play. In the procession of the soul from within outward, it enlarges its circles ever, like the pebble thrown into the pond, or the light proceeding from an orb. The rays of the soul alight first on things nearest, on every utensil and toy, on nurses and domestics, on the house, and yard, and passengers, on the circle of household acquaintance, on politics, and geography, and history. But things are ever grouping themselves according to higher or more interior laws. Neighbourhood, size, numbers, habits, persons, lose by degrees their power over us. Cause and effect, real affinities, the longing for harmony between the soul and the circumstance, the progressive, idealizing instinct, predominate later, and the step backward from the higher to the lower relations is impossible. Thus even love, which is the deification of persons, must become more impersonal every day. Of this at first it gives no hint. Little think the youth and maiden who are glancing at each other across crowded rooms, with eyes so full of mutual intelligence, of the precious fruit long hereafter to proceed from this new, quite external stimulus. The work of vegetation begins first in the irritability of the bark and leaf-buds. From exchanging glances, they advance to acts of courtesy, of gallantry, then to fiery passion, to plighting troth, and marriage. Passion beholds its object as a perfect unit. The soul is wholly embodied, and the body is wholly ensouled.

> "Her pure and eloquent blood
> Spoke in her cheeks, and so distinctly
> wrought,

That one might almost say her body
thought."

Romeo, if dead, should be cut up into little stars to make the heavens fine. Life, with this pair, has no other aim, asks no more, than Juliet,—than Romeo. Night, day, studies, talents, kingdoms, religion, are all contained in this form full of soul, in this soul which is all form. The lovers delight in endearments, in avowals of love, in comparisons of their regards. When alone, they solace themselves with the remembered image of the other. Does that other see the same star, the same melting cloud, read the same book, feel the same emotion, that now delight me? They try and weigh their affection, and, adding up costly advantages, friends, opportunities, properties, exult in discovering that willingly, joyfully, they would give all as a ransom for the beautiful, the beloved head, not one hair of which shall be harmed. But the lot of humanity is on these children. Danger, sorrow, and pain arrive to them, as to all. Love prays. It makes covenants with Eternal Power in behalf of this dear mate. The union which is thus effected, and which adds a new value to every atom in nature, for it transmutes every thread throughout the whole web of relation into a golden ray, and bathes the soul in a new and sweeter element, is yet a temporary state. Not always can flowers, pearls, poetry, protestations, nor even home in another heart, content the awful soul that dwells in clay. It arouses itself at last from these endearments, as toys, and puts on the harness, and aspires to vast and universal aims. The soul which is in the soul of each, craving a perfect beatitude, detects incongruities, defects, and disproportion in the behaviour of the other. Hence arise surprise, expostulation, and pain. Yet that which drew them to each other was signs of loveliness, signs of virtue; and these virtues are there, however eclipsed. They appear and reappear, and continue to attract; but the regard changes, quits the sign, and attaches to the substance. This repairs the wounded affection. Meantime, as life wears on, it proves a game of permutation and combination of all possible positions of the parties, to employ all the resources of each, and acquaint each with the strength and weakness of the other. For it is the nature and end of this relation, that they should represent the human race to each other. All that is in the world, which is or ought to be known, is cunningly wrought into the texture of man, of woman.

"The person love does to us fit,
Like manna, has the taste of all in it."

The world rolls; the circumstances vary every hour. The angels that inhabit this temple of the body appear at the windows, and the gnomes and vices also. By all the virtues they are united. If there be virtue, all the vices are known as such; they confess and flee. Their once flaming regard is sobered by time in either breast, and, losing in violence what it gains in extent, it becomes a thorough good understanding. They resign each other, without complaint, to the good offices which man and woman are severally appointed to discharge in time, and exchange the passion which once could not lose sight of its object, for a cheerful, disengaged furtherance, whether present or absent, of each other's designs. At last they discover that all which at first drew them together,—those once sacred features, that magical play of charms,—was deciduous, had a prospective end, like the scaffolding by which the house was built; and the purification of the intellect and the heart, from year to year, is the real marriage, foreseen and prepared from the first, and wholly above their consciousness. Looking at these aims with which two persons, a man and a woman, so variously and correlatively gifted, are shut up in one house to spend in the nuptial society forty or fifty years, I do not wonder at the emphasis with which the heart prophesies this crisis from early infancy, at the profuse beauty with which the instincts deck the nuptial bower, and nature, and intellect, and art emulate each other in the gifts and the melody they bring to the epithalamium.

Thus are we put in training for a love which knows not sex, nor person, nor partiality, but which seeks virtue and wisdom everywhere, to the end of increasing virtue and wisdom. We are by nature observers, and thereby learners. That is our permanent state. But we are often made to feel that our affections are but tents of a night. Though slowly and with pain, the objects of the affections change, as the objects of thought do. There are moments when the affections rule and absorb the man, and make his happiness dependent on a person or persons. But in health the mind is presently seen again,—its overarching vault, bright with galaxies of immutable lights, and the warm loves and fears that swept over us as clouds, must lose their finite character and blend with God, to attain their own perfection. But we need not fear that we can lose any thing by the progress of the soul. The soul may be trusted to the end. That which is so beautiful and attractive as these relations must be succeeded and supplanted only by what is more beautiful, and so on for ever.

Why?

PLATO

from Symposium

Aristophanes professed to open another vein of discourse; he had a mind to praise Love in another way, unlike that either of Pausanias or Eryximachus. Mankind, he said, judging by their neglect of him, have never, as I think, at all understood the power of Love. For if they had understood him they would surely have built noble temples and altars, and offered solemn sacrifices in his honour; but this is not done, and most certainly ought to be done: since of all the gods he is the best friend of men, the helper and the healer of the ills which are the great impediment to the happiness of the race. I will try to describe his power to you, and you shall teach the rest of the world what I am teaching you. In the first place, let me treat of the nature of man and what has happened to it; for the original human nature was not like the present, but different. The sexes were not two as they are now, but originally three in number; there was man, woman, and the union of the two, having a name corresponding to this double nature, which had once a real existence, but is now lost, and the word 'Androgynous' is only preserved as a term of reproach. In the second place, the primeval man was round, his back and sides forming a circle; and he had four hands and four feet, one head with two faces, looking opposite ways, set on a round neck and precisely alike; also four ears, two privy members, and the remainder to correspond. He could walk upright as men now do, backwards or forwards as he pleased, and he could also roll over and over at a great pace, turning on his four hands and four feet, eight in all, like tumblers going over and over with their legs in the air; this was when he wanted to run fast. Now the sexes were three, and such as I have described them; because the sun, moon, and earth are three; and the man was originally the child of the sun, the woman of the earth, and the man-woman of the moon, which is made up of sun and earth, and they were all round and moved round and round like their parents. Terrible was their might and strength, and the thoughts of their hearts were great, and they made an attack upon the gods; of them is told the tale of Otys and Ephialtes who, as Homer says, dared to scale heaven, and would have laid hands upon the gods. Doubt reigned in the celestial councils. Should they kill them and annihilate the race with thunderbolts, as they had done the giants, then there would be an end of the sacrifices and worship which men offered to them; but, on the other hand, the gods could not suffer their insolence to be unrestrained. At last, after a good deal of reflection, Zeus discovered a way. He said: 'Methinks I have a plan which will humble their pride and improve their manners; men shall continue to exist, but I will cut them in two and then they will be diminished in strength and increased in numbers; this will have the advantage of making them more profitable to us. They shall walk upright on two legs, and if they continue insolent and will not be quiet, I will split them again and they shall hop about on a single leg.' He spoke and cut men in two, like a sorb-apple which is halved for pickling, or as you might divide an egg with a hair; and as he cut them one after another, he bade Apollo give the face and the half of the neck a turn in order that the man might contemplate the section of himself: he would thus learn a lesson of humility. Apollo was also bidden to heal their wounds and compose their forms. So he gave a turn to the face and pulled the skin from the sides all over that which in our language is called the belly, like the purses which draw in, and he made one mouth at the centre, which he fastened in a knot (the same which is called the navel); he also moulded the breast and took out most of the wrinkles, much as a shoemaker might smooth leather upon a last; he left a few, however, in the region of the belly and navel, as a memorial of the primeval state. After the division the two parts of man, each desiring his other half, came together, and throwing their arms about one another, entwined in mutual embraces, longing to grow into one, they were on the point of dying from hunger and self-neglect, because they did not like to do anything apart; and when one of the halves died and the other survived, the survivor sought another mate, man or woman as we call them,—being the sections of entire men or women,—and clung to that. They were being destroyed, when Zeus in pity of them invented a new plan: he turned the parts of generation round to the front, for this had not been always their position, and they sowed the seed no longer as hitherto like grasshoppers in the ground, but in one another; and after the transposition the male generated in the female in order that by the mutual embraces of man and woman they might breed, and the race might continue; or if man came to man they might be satisfied, and rest, and go their ways to the business of life: so ancient is the desire of one another which is implanted in us, reuniting our original nature, making one of two, and healing the state of man. Each of us when separated, having one side only, like a flat fish, is but the indenture of a man, and he is always looking for his other half. Men who are a section of that double nature which was once called Androgynous are lovers of women; adulterers are generally of this breed, and also adulterous women who lust after men: the women who are a section of the woman do not care for men, but have female attachments; the female companions are of this sort. But they who are a section of the male follow the male, and while they are young, being slices of the original man, they hang about men and embrace them, and they are themselves the best of boys and youths, because they have the most manly nature. Some indeed assert that they are shameless, but this is not true; for they do not act thus from any want of shame, but because they are valiant and manly, and have a manly countenance, and they embrace that which is like them. And these when they grow up become our statesmen, and these only, which is a great proof of the truth of what I am saying. When they reach manhood they are lovers of youth, and are not naturally inclined to marry or beget children,—if at all, they do so only in obedience to the law; but they are satisfied if they may be allowed to live with one another unwedded; and such a nature is prone to love and ready to return love, always embracing that which is akin to him. And when one of them meets with his other half, the actual half of himself, whether he be a lover of youth or a lover of another sort, the pair are lost in an amazement of love and friendship and intimacy, and one will not be out of the other's sight, as I may say, even for a moment: these are the people who pass their whole lives together; yet they could not explain what they desire of one another. For the intense yearning which each of them has towards the other does not appear to be the desire of lover's intercourse, but of something else which the soul of either evidently desires and cannot tell, and of which she has only a dark and doubtful presentiment. Suppose Hephaestus, with his instruments, to come to the pair who are lying side by side and to say to them, 'What do you two people want of one another?' they would be unable to explain. And suppose further, that when he saw their perplexity he said: 'Do you desire to be wholly one; always day and night to be in one another's company? for if this is what you desire, I am ready to melt you into one and let you grow together, so that being two you shall become one, and while you live live a common life as if you were a single man, and after your death in the world below still be one departed soul instead of two—I ask whether this is what you lovingly desire, and whether you are satisfied to attain this?'—there is not a man of them who when he heard the proposal would deny or would not acknowledge that this meeting and melting into one another, this becoming one instead of two, was the very expression of his ancient need. And the reason is that human nature was originally one and we were a whole, and the desire and pursuit of the whole is called love. There was a time, I say, when we were one, but now because of the wickedness of mankind God has dispersed us, as the Arcadians were dispersed into villages by the Lacedaemonians. And if we are not obedient to the gods, there is a danger that we shall be split up again and go about in basso-relievo, like the profile figures having only half a nose which are sculptured on monuments, and that we shall be like tallies. Wherefore let us exhort all men to piety, that we may avoid evil, and obtain the good, of which Love is to us the lord and minister; and let no one oppose him—he is the enemy of the gods who opposes him. For if we are friends of the God and at peace with him we shall find our own true loves, which rarely happens in this world at present. I am serious, and therefore I must beg Eryximachus not to make fun or to find any allusion in what I am saying to Pausanias and Agathon, who, as I suspect, are both of the manly nature, and belong to the class which I have been describing. But my words have a wider application—they include men and women everywhere; and I believe that if our loves were perfectly accomplished, and each one returning to his primeval nature had his original true love, then our race would be happy. And if this would be best of all, the best in the next degree and under present circumstances must be the nearest approach to such an union; and that will be the attainment of a congenial love. Wherefore, if we would praise him who has given to us the benefit, we must praise the god Love, who is our greatest benefactor, both leading us in this life back to our own nature, and giving us high hopes for the future, for he promises that if we are pious, he will restore us to our original state, and heal us and make us happy and blessed. This, Eryximachus, is my discourse of love, which, although different to yours, I must beg you to leave unassailed by the shafts of your ridicule, in order that each may have his turn; each, or rather either, for Agathon and Socrates are the only ones left.

ROBERT LOUIS STEVENSON

On Falling in Love

"Lord, what fools these mortals be!"

There is only one event in life which really astonishes a man and startles him out of his prepared opinions. Everything else befalls him very much as he expected. Event succeeds to event, with an agreeable variety indeed, but with little that is either startling or intense; they form together no more than a sort of background, or running accompaniment to the man's own reflections; and he falls naturally into a cool, curious, and smiling habit of mind, and builds himself up in a conception of life which expects to-morrow to be after the pattern of to-day and yesterday. He may be accustomed to the vagaries of his friends and acquaintances under the influence of love. He may sometimes look forward to it for himself with an incomprehensible expectation. But it is a subject in which neither intuition nor the behaviour of others will help the philosopher to the truth. There is probably nothing rightly thought or rightly written on this matter of love that is not a piece of the person's experience. I remember an anecdote of a well-known French theorist, who was debating a point eagerly in his *cénacle*. It was objected against him that he had never experienced love. Whereupon he arose, left the society, and made it a point not to return to it until he considered that he had supplied the defect. "Now," he remarked, on entering, "now I am in a position to continue the discussion." Perhaps he had not penetrated very deeply into the subject after all; but the story indicates right thinking, and may serve as an apologue to readers of this essay.

When at last the scales fall from his eyes, it is not without something of the nature of dismay that the man finds himself in such changed conditions. He has to deal with commanding emotions instead of the easy dislikes and preferences in which he has hitherto passed his days; and he recognizes capabilities for pain and pleasure of which he had not yet suspected the existence.

Falling in love is the one illogical adventure, the one thing of which we are tempted to think as supernatural, in our trite and reasonable world. The effect is out of all proportion with the cause. Two persons, neither of them, it may be, very amiable or very beautiful, meet, speak a little, and look a little into each other's eyes. That has been done a dozen or so of times in the experience of either with no great result. But on this occasion all is different. They fall at once into that state in which another person becomes to us the very gist and centrepoint of God's creation, and demolishes our laborious theories with a smile; in which our ideas are so bound up with the one master-thought that even the trivial cares of our own person become so many acts of devotion, and the love of life itself is translated into a wish to remain in the same world with so precious and desirable a fellow-creature. And all the while their acquaintances look on in stupor, and ask each other, with almost passionate emphasis, what so-and-so can see in that woman, or such-an-one in that man? I am sure, gentlemen, I cannot tell you. For my part, I cannot think what the women mean. It might be very well, if the Apollo Belvedere should suddenly glow all over into life, and step forward from the pedestal with that godlike air of his. But of the misbegotten changelings who call themselves men, and prate intolerably over dinner-tables, I never saw one who seemed worthy to inspire love—no, nor read of any, except Leonardo da Vinci, and perhaps Goethe in his youth. About women I entertain a somewhat different opinion; but there, I have the misfortune to be a man.

There are many matters in which you may waylay Destiny, and bid him stand and deliver. Hard work, high thinking, adventurous excitement, and a great deal more that forms a part of this or the other person's spiritual bill of fare, are within the reach of almost any one who can dare a little and be patient. But it is by no means in the way of every one to fall in love. You know the difficulty Shakespeare was put into when Queen Elizabeth asked him to show Falstaff in love. I do not believe that Henry Fielding was ever in love. Scott, if it were not for a passage or two in *Rob Roy*, would give me very much the same effect. These are great names and (what is more to the purpose) strong, healthy, high-strung, and generous natures, of whom the reverse might have been expected. As for the innumerable army of anæmic and tailorish persons who occupy the face of this planet with so much propriety, it is palpably absurd to imagine them in any such situation as a love-affair. A wet rag goes safely by the fire; and if a man is blind, he cannot expect to be much impressed by romantic scenery. Apart from all this, many lovable people miss each other in the world, or meet under some unfavourable star. There is the nice and critical moment of declaration to be got over. From timidity or lack of opportunity a good half of possible love cases never get so far, and at least another quarter do there cease and determine. A very adroit person, to be sure, manages to prepare the way and out with his declaration in the nick of time. And then there is a fine solid sort of man, who goes on from snub to snub; and if he has to declare forty times, will continue imperturbably declaring, amid the astonished consideration of men and angels, until he has a favourable answer. I dare say, if one were a woman, one would like to marry a man who was capable of doing this, but not quite one who had done so. It is just a little bit abject, and somehow just a little bit gross; and marriages in which one of the parties has been thus battered into consent scarcely form agreeable subjects for meditation. Love should run out to meet love with open arms. Indeed, the ideal story is that of two people who go into love step for step, with a fluttered consciousness, like a pair of children venturing together into a dark room. From the first moment when they see each other, with a pang of curiosity, through stage after stage of growing pleasure and embarrassment, they can read the expression of their own trouble in each other's eyes. There is here no declaration properly so called; the feeling is so plainly shared, that as soon as the man knows what it is in his own heart, he is sure of what it is in the woman's.

This simple accident of falling in love is as beneficial as it is astonishing. It arrests the petrifying influence of years, disproves cold-blooded and cynical conclusions, and awakens dormant sensibilities. Hitherto the man had found it a good policy to disbelieve the existence of any enjoyment which was out of his reach; and thus he turned his back upon the strong sunny parts of nature, and accustomed himself to look exclusively on what was common and dull. He accepted a prose ideal, let himself go blind of many sympathies by disuse; and if he were young and witty, or beautiful, wilfully forewent these advantages. He joined himself to the following of what, in the old mythology of love, was prettily called *nonchaloir*; and in an odd mixture of feelings, a fling of self-respect, a preference for selfish liberty, and a great dash of that fear with which good people regard serious interests, kept himself back from the straightforward course of life among certain selected activities. And now, all of a sudden, he is unhorsed, like St. Paul, from his infidel affectation. His heart, which has been ticking accurate seconds for the last year, gives a bound and begins to beat high and irregularly in his breast. It seems as if he had never heard or felt or seen until that moment; and by the report of his memory, he must have lived his past life between sleep and waking, or with the preoccupied attention of a brown study. He is practically incommoded by the generosity of his feelings, smiles much when he is alone, and develops a habit of looking rather blankly upon the moon and stars. But it is not at all within the province of a prose essayist to give a picture of this hyperbolical frame of mind; and the thing has been done already, and that to admiration. In *Adelaide*, in Tennyson's *Maud*, and in some of Heine's songs, you get the absolute expression of this midsummer spirit. Romeo and Juliet were very much in love; although they tell me some German critics are of a different opinion, probably the same who would have us think Mercutio a dull fellow. Poor Antony was in love, and no mistake. That lay figure Marius, in *Les Misérables*, is also a genuine case in his own way, and worth observation. A good many of George Sand's people are thoroughly in love; and so are a good many of George Meredith's. Altogether, there is plenty to read on the subject. If the root of the matter be in him, and if he has the requisite chords to set in vibration, a young man may occasionally enter, with the key of art, into that land of Beulah which is upon the borders of Heaven and within sight of the City of Love. There let him sit awhile to hatch delightful hopes and perilous illusions.

One thing that accompanies the passion in its first blush is certainly difficult to explain. It comes (I do not quite see how) that from having a very supreme sense of pleasure in all parts of life—in lying down to sleep, in waking, in motion, in breathing, in continuing to be—the lover begins to regard his happiness as beneficial for the rest of the world, and highly meritorious in himself. Our race has never been able contentedly to suppose that the noise of its wars, conducted by a few young gentlemen in a corner of an inconsiderable star, does not re-echo among the courts of Heaven with quite a formidable effect. In much the same taste, when people find a great to-do in their own breasts, they imagine it must have some influence in their neighbourhood. The presence of the two lovers is so enchanting to each other that it seems as if it must be the best thing possible for everybody else. They are half inclined to fancy it is because of them and their love that the sky is blue and the sun shines. And certainly the weather is usually fine while people are courting . . . In point of fact, although the happy man feels very kindly towards others of his own sex, there is apt to be something too much of the magnifico in his demeanour. If people grow presuming and self-important over such matters as a dukedom or the Holy See, they will scarcely support the dizziest elevation in life without some suspicion of a strut; and the dizziest elevation is to love and be loved in return. Consequently, accepted lovers are a trifle condescending in their address to other men. An overweening sense of the passion and importance of life hardly conduces to simplicity of manner. To women, they feel very nobly, very purely, and very generously, as if they were so many Joan-of-Arcs; but this does not come out in their behaviour; and they treat them to Grandisonian airs marked with a suspicion of fatuity. I am not quite certain that women do not like this sort of thing; but really, after having bemused myself over *Daniel Deronda*, I have given up trying to understand what they like.

If it did nothing else, this sublime and ridiculous superstition, that the pleasure of the pair is somehow blessed to others, and everybody is made happier in their happiness, would serve at least to keep love generous and great-hearted. Nor is it quite a baseless superstition after all. Other lovers are hugely interested. They strike the nicest balance between pity and approval, when they see people aping the greatness of their own sentiments. It is an understood thing in the play, that while the young gentlefolk are courting on the terrace, a rough flirtation is being carried on, and a light, trivial sort of love is growing up, between the footman and the singing chambermaid. As people are generally cast for the leading parts in their own imaginations, the reader can apply the parallel to real life without much chance of going wrong. In short, they are quite sure this other love-affair is not so deep-seated as their own, but they like dearly to see it going forward. And love, considered as a spectacle, must have attractions for many who are not of the confraternity. The sentimental old maid is a commonplace of the novelists; and he must be rather a poor sort of human being, to be sure, who can look on at this pretty madness without indulgence and sympathy. For nature commends itself to people with a most insinuating art; the busiest is now and again arrested by a great sunset; and you may be as pacific or as cold-blooded as you will, but you cannot help some emotion when you read of well-disputed battles, or meet a pair of lovers in the lane.

Certainly, whatever it may be with regard to the world at large, this idea of beneficent pleasure is true as between the sweethearts. To do good and communicate is the lover's grand intention. It is the happiness of the other that makes his own most intense gratification. It is not possible to disentangle the different emotions, the pride, humility, pity and passion, which are excited by a look of happy love or an unexpected caress. To make oneself beautiful, to dress the hair, to excel in talk, to do anything and all things that puff out the character and attributes and make them imposing in the eyes of others, is not only to magnify one's self, but to offer the most delicate homage at the same time. And it is in this latter intention that they are done by lovers; for the essence of love is kindness; and indeed it may be best defined as passionate kindness: kindness, so to speak, run mad and become importunate and violent. Vanity in a merely personal sense exists no longer. The lover takes a perilous pleasure in privately displaying his weak points and having them, one after another, accepted and condoned. He wishes to be assured that he is not loved for this or that good quality, but for himself, or something as like himself as he can contrive to set forward. For, although it may have been a very difficult thing to paint the marriage of Cana, or write the fourth act of Antony and Cleopatra, there is a more difficult piece of art before every one in this world who cares to set about explaining his own character to others. Words and acts are easily wrenched from their true significance; and they are all the language we have to come and go upon. A pitiful job we make of it, as a rule. For better or worse, people mistake our meaning and take our emotions at a wrong valuation. And generally we rest pretty content with our failures; we are content to be misapprehended by cackling flirts; but when once a man is moonstruck with this affection of love, he makes it a point of honour to clear such dubieties away. He cannot have the Best of her Sex misled upon a point of this importance; and his pride revolts at being loved in a mistake.

He discovers a great reluctance to return on former periods of his life. To all that has not been shared with her, rights and duties, bygone fortunes and dispositions, he can look back only by a difficult and repugnant effort of the will. That he should have wasted some years in ignorance of what alone was really important, that he may have entertained the thought of other women with any show of complacency, is a burthen almost too heavy for his self-respect. But it is the thought of another past that rankles in his spirit like a poisoned wound. That he himself made a fashion of being alive in the bald, beggarly days before a certain meeting, is deplorable enough in all good conscience. But that She should have permitted herself the same liberty seems inconsistent with a Divine providence.

A great many people run down jealousy, on the score that it is an artificial feeling, as well as practically inconvenient. This is scarcely fair; for the feeling on which it merely attends, like an ill-humoured courtier, is itself artificial in exactly the same sense and to the same degree. I suppose what is meant by that objection is that jealousy has not always been a character of man; formed no part of that very modest kit of sentiments with which he is supposed to have begun the world; but waited to make its appearance in better days and among richer natures. And this is equally true of love, and friendship, and love of country, and delight in what they call the beauties of nature, and most other things worth having. Love, in particular, will not endure any historical scrutiny: to all who have fallen across it, it is one of the most incontestable facts in the world; but if you begin to ask what it was in other periods and countries, in Greece for instance, the strangest doubts begin to spring up, and everything seems so vague and changing that a dream is logical in comparison. Jealousy, at any rate, is one of the consequences of love; you may like it or not, at pleasure; but there it is.

It is not exactly jealousy, however, that we feel when we reflect on the past of those we love. A bundle of letters found after years of happy union creates no sense of insecurity in the present; and yet it will pain a man sharply. The two people entertain no vulgar doubt of each other: but this pre-existence of both occurs to the mind as something indelicate. To be altogether right, they should have had twin birth together, at the same moment with the feeling that unites them. Then indeed it would be simple and perfect and without reserve or afterthought. Then they would understand each other with a fulness impossible otherwise. There would be no barrier between them of associations that cannot be imparted.

They would be led into none of those comparisons that send the blood back to the heart. And they would know that there had been no time lost, and they had been together as much as was possible. For besides terror for the separation that must follow some time or other in the future, men feel anger, and something like remorse, when they think of that other separation which endured until they met. Some one has written that love makes people believe in immortality, because there seems not to be room enough in life for so great a tenderness, and it is inconceivable that the most masterful of our emotions should have no more than the spare moments of a few years. Indeed, it seems strange; but if we call to mind analogies, we can hardly regard it as impossible.

"The blind bow-boy," who smiles upon us from the end of terraces in old Dutch gardens, laughingly hails his bird-bolts among a fleeting generation. But for as fast as ever he shoots, the game dissolves and disappears into eternity from under his falling arrows; this one is gone ere he is struck; the other has but time to make one gesture and give one passionate cry; and they are all the things of a moment. When the generation is gone, when the play is over, when the thirty years' panorama has been withdrawn in tatters from the stage of the world, we may ask what has become of these great, weighty, and undying loves, and the sweethearts who despised mortal conditions in a fine credulity; and they can only show us a few songs in a bygone taste, a few actions worth remembering, and a few children who have retained some happy stamp from the disposition of their parents.

FRANCIS BACON

Cupid, Or an Atom

Explained Of The Corpuscular Philosophy

The particulars related by the poets of Cupid, or Love, do not properly agree to the same person, yet they differ only so far, that if the confusion of persons be rejected, the correspondence may hold. They say, that Love was the most ancient of all the gods, and existed before every thing else, except Chaos, which is held coeval therewith. But for Chaos, the ancients never paid divine honors, nor gave the title of a god thereto. Love is represented absolutely without progenitor, excepting only that he is said to have proceeded from the egg of Nox; but that himself begot the gods, and all things else, on Chaos. His attributes are four; viz: 1, perpetual infancy; 2, blindness; 3, nakedness; and 4, archery.

There was also another Cupid, or Love, the

youngest son of the gods, born of Venus; and upon him the attributes of the elder are transferred, with some degree of correspondence.

Explanation.—This fable points at, and enters, the cradle of nature. Love seems to be the appetite, or incentive, of the primitive matter; or, to speak more distinctly, the natural motion, or moving principle, of the original corpuscles, or atoms; this being the most ancient and only power that made and wrought all things out of matter. It is absolutely without parent, that is, without cause; for causes are as parents to effects; but this power or efficacy could have no natural cause; for, excepting God, nothing was before it; and therefore it could have no efficient in nature. And as nothing is more inward with nature, it can neither be a genus nor a form; and therefore, whatever it is, it must be somewhat positive, though inexpressible. And if it were possible to conceive its modus and process, yet it could not be known from its cause, as being, next to God, the cause of causes, and itself without a cause. And, perhaps, we are not to hope that the modus of it should fall, or be comprehended, under human inquiry. Whence it is properly feigned to be the egg of Nox, or laid in the dark.

The divine philosopher declares, that "God has made every thing beautiful in its season; and has given over the world to our disputes and inquiries; but that man cannot find out the work which God has wrought, from its beginning up to its end." Thus the summary or collective law of nature, or the principle of love, impressed by God upon the original particles of all things, so as to make them attack each other and come together, by the repetition and multiplication whereof all the variety in the universe is produced, can scarce possibly find full admittance into the thoughts of men, though some faint notion may be had thereof. The Greek philosophy is subtile, and busied in discovering the material principles of things, but negligent and languid in discovering the principles of motion, in which the energy and efficacy of every operation consists. And here the Greek philosophers seem perfectly blind and childish; for the opinion of the Peripatetics, as to the stimulus of matter, by privation, is little more than words, or rather sound than signification. And they who refer it to God, though they do well therein, yet they do it by a start, and not by proper degrees of assent; for doubtless there is one summary, or capital law, in which nature meets, subordinate to God, viz: the law mentioned in the passage above quoted from Solomon; or the work which God has wrought from its beginning to its end.

Democritus, who further considered this subject, having first supposed an atom, or corpuscle, of some dimension or figure, attributed thereto an appetite, desire, or first motion simply, and another comparatively, imagining that all things properly tended to the centre of the world; those containing more matter falling faster to the centre, and thereby removing, and in the shock driving away, such as held less. But this is a slender conceit, and regards too few particulars; for neither the revolutions of the celestial bodies, nor the contractions and expansions of things, can be reduced to this principle. And for the opinion of Epicurus, as to the declination and fortuitous agitation of atoms, this only brings the matter back again to a trifle, and wraps it up in ignorance and night.

Cupid is elegantly drawn a perpetual child; for compounds are larger things, and have their periods of age; but the first seeds or atoms of bodies are small, and remain in a perpetual infant state.

He is again justly represented naked; as all compounds may properly be said to be dressed and clothed, or to assume a personage; whence nothing remains truly naked, but the original particles of things.

The blindness of Cupid contains a deep allegory; for this same Cupid, Love, or appetite of the world, seems to have very little foresight, but directs his steps and motions conformably to what he finds next him, as blind men do when they feel out their way; which renders the divine and overruling Providence and foresight the more surprising; as by a certain steady law, it brings such a beautiful order and regularity of things out of what seems extremely casual, void of design, and, as it were, really blind.

The last attribute of Cupid is archery, viz: a virtue or power operating at a distance; for every thing that operates at a distance may seem, as it were, to dart, or shoot with arrows. And whoever allows of atoms and vacuity, necessarily supposes that the virtue of atoms operates at a distance; for without this operation, no motion could be excited, on account of the vacuum interposing, but all things would remain sluggish and unmoved.

As to the other Cupid, he is properly said to be the youngest son of the gods, as his power could not take place before the formation of species, or particular bodies. The description given us of him transfers the allegory to morality, though he still retains some resemblance with the ancient Cupid; for as Venus universally excites the affection of association, and the desire of procreation, her son Cupid applies the affection to individuals; so that the general disposition proceeds from Venus, but the more close sympathy from Cupid. The former depends upon a near approximation of causes, but the latter upon deeper, more necessitating and uncontrollable principles, as if they proceeded from the ancient Cupid, on whom all exquisite sympathies depend.

EMMA GOLDMAN

Marriage and Love

The popular notion about marriage and love is that they are synonymous, that they spring from the same motives, and cover the same human needs. Like most popular notions this also rests not on actual facts, but on superstition.

Marriage and love have nothing in common; they are as far apart as the poles; are, in fact, antagonistic to each other. No doubt some marriages have been the result of love. Not, however, because love could assert itself only in marriage; much rather is it because few people can completely outgrow a convention. There are today large numbers of men and women to whom marriage is naught but a farce, but who submit to it for the sake of public opinion. At any rate, while it is true that some marriages are based on love, and while it is equally true that in some cases love continues in married life, I maintain that it does so regardless of marriage, and not because of it.

On the other hand, it is utterly false that love results from marriage. On rare occasions one does hear of a miraculous case of a married couple falling in love after marriage, but on close examination it will be found that it is a mere adjustment to the inevitable. Certainly the growing-used to each other is far away from the spontaneity, the intensity, and beauty of love, without which the intimacy of marriage must prove degrading to both the woman and the man.

Marriage is primarily an economic arrangement, an insurance pact. It differs from the ordinary life insurance agreement only in that it is more binding, more exacting. Its returns are insignificantly small compared with the investments. In taking out an insurance policy one pays for it in dollars and cents, always at liberty to discontinue payments. If, however, woman's premium is a husband, she pays for it with her name, her privacy, her self-respect, her very life, "until death doth part." Moreover, the marriage insurance condemns her to life-long dependency, to parasitism, to complete uselessness, individual as well as social. Man, too, pays his toll, but as his sphere is wider, marriage does not limit him as much as woman. He feels his chains more in an economic sense.

Thus Dante's motto over Inferno applies with equal force to marriage. "Ye who enter here leave all hope behind."

That marriage is a failure none but the very stupid will deny. One has but to glance over the statistics of divorce to realize how bitter a failure marriage really is. Nor will the stereotyped Philistine argument that the laxity of divorce laws and the growing looseness of woman account for the fact that: first, every twelfth marriage ends in divorce; second, that since 1870 divorces have increased from 28 to 73 for every hundred thousand population; third, that adultery, since 1867, as ground for divorce, has increased 270.8 per cent.; fourth, that desertion increased 369.8 per cent.

Added to these startling figures is a vast amount of material, dramatic and literary, further elucidating this subject. Robert Herrick, in *Together*; Pinero, in *Mid-Channel*; Eugene Walter, in *Paid in Full*, and scores of other writers are discussing the barrenness, the monotony, the sordidness, the inadequacy of marriage as a factor for harmony and understanding.

The thoughtful social student will not content

himself with the popular superficial excuse for this phenomenon. He will have to dig down deeper into the very life of the sexes to know why marriage proves so disastrous.

Edward Carpenter says that behind every marriage stands the life-long environment of the two sexes; an environment so different from each other that man and woman must remain strangers. Separated by an insurmountable wall of superstition, custom, and habit, marriage has not the potentiality of developing knowledge of, and respect for, each other, without which every union is doomed to failure.

Henrik Ibsen, the hater of all social shams, was probably the first to realize this great truth. Nora leaves her husband, not—as the stupid critic would have it—because she is tired of her responsibilities or feels the need of woman's rights, but because she has come to know that for eight years she had lived with a stranger and borne him children. Can there be anything more humiliating, more degrading than a lifelong proximity between two strangers? No need for the woman to know anything of the man, save his income. As to the knowledge of the woman—what is there to know except that she has a pleasing appearance? We have not yet outgrown the theologic myth that woman has no soul, that she is a mere appendix to man, made out of his rib just for the convenience of the gentleman who was so strong that he was afraid of his own shadow.

Perchance the poor quality of the material whence woman comes is responsible for her inferiority. At any rate, woman has no soul—what is there to know about her? Besides, the less soul a woman has the greater her asset as a wife, the more readily will she absorb herself in her husband. It is this slavish acquiescence to man's superiority that has kept the marriage institution seemingly intact for so long a period. Now that woman is coming into her own, now that she is actually growing aware of herself as a being outside of the master's grace, the sacred institution of marriage is gradually being undermined, and no amount of sentimental lamentation can stay it.

From infancy, almost, the average girl is told that marriage is her ultimate goal; therefore her training and education must be directed towards that end. Like the mute beast fattened for slaughter, she is prepared for that. Yet, strange to say, she is allowed to know much less about her function as wife and mother than the ordinary artisan of his trade. It is indecent and filthy for a respectable girl to know anything of the marital relation. Oh, for the inconsistency of respectability, that needs the marriage vow to turn something which is filthy into the purest and most sacred arrangement that none dare question or criticize. Yet that is exactly the attitude of the average upholder of marriage. The prospective wife and mother is kept in complete ignorance of her only asset in the competitive field—sex. Thus she enters into life-long relations with a man only to find herself shocked, repelled, outraged beyond measure by the most natural and healthy instinct, sex. It is safe to say that a large percentage of the unhappiness, misery, distress, and physical suffering of matrimony is due to the criminal ignorance in sex matters that is being extolled as a great virtue. Nor is it at all an exaggeration when I say that more than one home has been broken up because of this deplorable fact.

If, however, woman is free and big enough to learn the mystery of sex without the sanction of State or Church, she will stand condemned as utterly unfit to become the wife of a "good" man, his goodness consisting of an empty brain and plenty of money. Can there be anything more outrageous than the idea that a healthy, grown woman, full of life and passion, must deny nature's demand, must subdue her most intense craving, undermine her health and break her spirit, must stunt her vision, abstain from the depth and glory of sex experience until a "good" man comes along to take her unto himself as a wife? That is precisely what marriage means. How can such an arrangement end except in failure? This is one, though not the least important, factor of marriage, which differentiates it from love.

Ours is a practical age. The time when Romeo and Juliet risked the wrath of their fathers for love, when Gretchen exposed herself to the gossip of her neighbors for love, is no more. If, on rare occasions, young people allow themselves the luxury of romance, they are taken in care by the elders, drilled and pounded until they become "sensible."

The moral lesson instilled in the girl is not whether the man has aroused her love, but rather is it, "How much?" The important and only God of practical American life: Can the man make a living? can he support a wife? That is the only thing that justifies marriage. Gradually this saturates every thought of the girl; her dreams are not of moonlight and kisses, of laughter and tears; she dreams of shopping tours and bargain counters. This soul poverty and sordidness are the elements inherent in the marriage institution. The State and the Church approve of no other ideal, simply because it is the one that necessitates the State and Church control of men and women.

Doubtless there are people who continue to consider love above dollars and cents. Particularly is this true of that class whom economic necessity has forced to become self-supporting. The tremendous change in woman's position, wrought by that mighty factor, is indeed phenomenal when we reflect that it is but a short time since she has entered the industrial arena. Six million women wage workers; six million women, who have the equal right with men to be exploited, to be robbed, to go on strike; aye, to starve even. Anything more, my lord? Yes, six million wage workers in every walk of life, from the highest brain work to the mines and railroad tracks; yes, even detectives and policemen. Surely the emancipation is complete.

Yet with all that, but a very small number of the vast army of women wage workers look upon work as a permanent issue, in the same light as does man. No matter how decrepit the latter, he has been taught to be independent, self-supporting. Oh, I know that no one is really independent in our economic treadmill; still, the poorest specimen of a man hates to be a parasite; to be known as such, at any rate.

The woman considers her position as worker transitory, to be thrown aside for the first bidder. That is why it is infinitely harder to organize women than men. "Why should I join a union? I am going to get married, to have a home." Has she not been taught from infancy to look upon that as her ultimate calling? She learns soon enough that the home, though not so large a prison as the factory, has more solid doors and bars. It has a keeper so faithful that naught can escape him. The most tragic part, however, is that the home no longer frees her from wage slavery; it only increases her task.

According to the latest statistics submitted before a Committee "on labor and wages, and congestion of population," ten per cent. of the wage workers in New York City alone are married, yet they must continue to work at the most poorly paid labor in the world. Add to this horrible aspect the drudgery of housework, and what remains of the protection and glory of the home? As a matter of fact, even the middle-class girl in marriage can not speak of her home, since it is the man who creates her sphere. It is not important whether the husband is a brute or a darling. What I wish to prove is that marriage guarantees woman a home only by the grace of her husband. There she moves about in *his* home, year after year, until her aspect of life and human affairs becomes as flat, narrow, and drab as her surroundings. Small wonder if she becomes a nag, petty, quarrelsome, gossipy, unbearable, thus driving the man from the house. She could not go, if she wanted to; there is no place to go. Besides, a short period of married life, of complete surrender of all faculties, absolutely incapacitates the average woman for the outside world. She becomes reckless in appearance, clumsy in her movements, dependent in her decisions, cowardly in her judgment, a weight and a bore, which most men grow to hate and despise. Wonderfully inspiring atmosphere for the bearing of life, is it not?

But the child, how is it to be protected, if not for marriage? After all, is not that the most important consideration? The sham, the hypocrisy of it! Marriage protecting the child, yet thousands of children destitute and homeless. Marriage protecting the child, yet orphan asylums and reformatories overcrowded, the Society for the Prevention of Cruelty to Children keeping busy in rescuing the little victims from "loving" parents, to place them under more loving care, the Gerry Society. Oh, the mockery of it!

Marriage may have the power to bring the horse to water, but has it ever made him drink? The law will place the father under arrest, and put him in convict's clothes; but has that ever stilled the hunger of the child? If the parent has no work, or if he hides his identity, what does marriage do then? It invokes the law to bring the man to "justice," to put him safely behind closed doors; his labor, however, goes not to the child, but to the State. The child receives but a blighted memory of its father's stripes.

As to the protection of the woman,—therein lies the curse of marriage. Not that it really protects her, but the very idea is so revolting, such an outrage and insult on life, so degrading to human dignity, as to forever condemn this parasitic institution.

It is like that other paternal arrangement—capitalism. It robs man of his birthright, stunts his growth, poisons his body, keeps him in ignorance, in poverty, and dependence, and then institutes charities that thrive on the last vestige of man's self-respect.

The institution of marriage makes a parasite of woman, an absolute dependent. It incapacitates her for life's struggle, annihilates her social consciousness, paralyzes her imagination, and then imposes its gracious protection, which is in reality a snare, a travesty on human character.

If motherhood is the highest fulfillment of woman's nature, what other protection does it need, save love and freedom? Marriage but defiles, outrages, and corrupts her fulfillment. Does it not say to woman, Only when you follow me shall you bring forth life? Does it not condemn her to the block, does it not degrade and shame her if she refuses to buy her right to motherhood by selling herself? Does not marriage only sanction motherhood, even though conceived in hatred, in compulsion? Yet, if motherhood be of free choice, of love, of ecstasy, of defiant passion, does it not place a crown of thorns upon an innocent head and carve in letters of blood the hideous epithet, Bastard? Were marriage to contain all the virtues claimed for it, its crimes against motherhood would exclude it forever from the realm of love.

Love, the strongest and deepest element in all life, the harbinger of hope, of joy, of ecstasy; love, the defier of all laws, of all conventions; love, the freest, the most powerful moulder of human destiny; how can such an all-compelling force be synonymous with that poor little State and Church-begotten weed, marriage?

Free love? As if love is anything but free! Man has bought brains, but all the millions in the world have failed to buy love. Man has subdued bodies, but all the power on earth has been unable to subdue love. Man has conquered whole nations, but all his armies could not conquer love. Man has chained and fettered the spirit, but he has been utterly helpless before love. High on a throne, with all the splendor and pomp his gold can command, man is yet poor and desolate, if love passes him by. And if it stays, the poorest hovel is radiant with warmth, with life and color. Thus love has the magic power to make of a beggar a king. Yes, love is free; it can dwell in no other atmosphere. In freedom it gives itself unreservedly, abundantly, completely. All the laws on the statutes, all the courts in the universe, cannot tear it from the soil, once love has taken root. If, however, the soil is sterile, how can marriage make it bear fruit? It is like the last desperate struggle of fleeting life against death.

Love needs no protection; it is its own protection. So long as love begets life no child is deserted, or hungry, or famished for the want of affection. I know this to be true. I know women who became mothers in freedom by the men they loved. Few children in wedlock enjoy the care, the protection, the devotion free motherhood is capable of bestowing.

The defenders of authority dread the advent of a free motherhood, lest it will rob them of their prey. Who would fight wars? Who would create wealth? Who would make the policeman, the jailer, if woman were to refuse the indiscriminate breeding of children? The race, the race! shouts the king, the president, the capitalist, the priest. The race must be preserved, though woman be degraded to a mere machine,—and the marriage institution is our only safety valve against the pernicious sex awakening of woman. But in vain these frantic efforts to maintain a state of bondage. In vain, too, the edicts of the Church, the mad attacks of rulers, in vain even the arm of the law. Woman no longer wants to be a party to the production of a race of sickly, feeble, decrepit, wretched human beings, who have neither the strength nor moral courage to throw off the yoke of poverty and slavery. Instead she desires fewer and better children, begotten and reared in love and through free choice; not by compulsion, as marriage imposes. Our pseudo-moralists have yet to learn the deep sense of responsibility toward the child, that love in freedom has awakened in the breast of woman. Rather would she forego forever the glory of motherhood than bring forth life in an atmosphere that breathes only destruction and death. And if she does become a mother, it is to give to the child the deepest and best her being can yield. To grow with the child is her motto; she knows that in that manner alone can she help build true manhood and womanhood.

Ibsen must have had a vision of a free mother, when, with a master stroke, he portrayed Mrs. Alving. She was the ideal mother because she had outgrown marriage and all its horrors, because she had broken her chains, and set her spirit free to soar until it returned a personality, regenerated and strong. Alas, it was too late to rescue her life's joy, her Oswald; but not too late to realize that love in freedom is the only condition of a beautiful life. Those who, like Mrs. Alving, have paid with blood and tears for their spiritual awakening, repudiate marriage as an imposition, a shallow, empty mockery. They know, whether love lasts but one brief span of time or for eternity, it is the only creative, inspiring, elevating basis for a new race, a new world.

In our present pygmy state love is indeed a stranger to most people. Misunderstood and shunned, it rarely takes root; or if it does, it soon withers and dies. Its delicate fiber can not endure the stress and strain of the daily grind. Its soul is too complex to adjust itself to the slimy woof of our social fabric. It weeps and moans and suffers with those who have need of it, yet lack the capacity to rise to love's summit.

Some day, some day men and women will rise, they will reach the mountain peak, they will meet big and strong and free, ready to receive, to partake, and to bask in the golden rays of love. What fancy, what imagination, what poetic genius can foresee even approximately the potentialities of such a force in the life of men and women. If the world is ever to give birth to true companionship and oneness, not marriage, but love will be the parent.

How?

STENDHAL

On Love

CHAPTER II
OF THE BIRTH OF LOVE

This is what takes place in the soul:—

1. Admiration.

2. A voice within says: "What pleasure to kiss, to be kissed."

3. Hope (3).

We study her perfections: this is the moment at which a woman should yield to realise the greatest possible physical pleasure. In the case even of the most reserved women, their eyes redden at the moment when hope is conceived: the passion is so strong, the pleasure so keen, that it betrays itself by striking signs.

4. Love is born.

To love—that is to have pleasure in seeing, touching, feeling, through all the senses and as near as possible, an object to be loved and that loves us.

5. The first crystallisation begins.

The lover delights in decking with a thousand perfections the woman of whose love he is sure: he dwells on all the details of his happiness with a satisfaction that is boundless. He is simply magnifying a superb bounty just fallen to him from heaven,—he has no knowledge of it but the assurance of its possession.

Leave the mind of a lover to its natural movements for twenty-four hours, and this is what you will find.

At the salt mines of Salzburg a branch stripped of its leaves by winter is thrown into the abandoned depths of the mine; taken out two or three months later it is covered with brilliant crystals; the smallest twigs, those no stouter than the leg of a sparrow, are arrayed with an infinity of sparkling, dazzling diamonds; it is impossible to recognise the original branch.

I call crystallisation the operation of the mind which, from everything which is presented to it, draws the conclusion that there are new perfections in the object of its love.

A traveller speaks of the freshness of the orange groves at Genoa, on the sea coast, during the scorching days of summer.—What pleasure to enjoy that freshness with her!

One of your friends breaks his arm in the hunting-field.—How sweet to be nursed by a woman you love! To be always with her, to see every moment her love for you, would make pain almost a blessing: and starting from the broken arm of your friend, you conclude with the absolute conviction of the angelic goodness of your mistress. In a word, it is enough to think of a perfection in order to see it in that which you love.

This phenomenon, which I venture to call crystallisation, is the product of human nature, which commands us to enjoy and sends warm blood rushing to our brain; it springs from the conviction that the pleasures of love increase with the perfections of its object, and from the idea: "She is mine." The savage has no time to go beyond the first step. He is delighted, but his mental activity is employed in following the flying deer in the forest, and with the flesh with which he must as soon as possible repair his forces, or fall beneath the axe of his enemy.

At the other pole of civilisation, I have no doubt that a sensitive woman may come to the point of feeling no physical pleasure but with the man she loves. It is the opposite with the savage. But among civilised peoples, woman has leisure at her disposal, while the savage is so pressed with necessary occupations that he is forced to treat his female as a beast of burden. If the females of many animals are more fortunate, it is because the subsistence of the males is more assured.

But let us leave the backwoods again for Paris. A man of passion sees all perfections in that which he loves. And yet his attention may still be distracted; for the soul has its surfeit of all that is uniform, even of perfect bliss.

This is what happens to distract his attention:—

6. Birth of Doubt.

After ten or twelve glances, or some other series of actions, which can last as well several days as one moment, hopes are first given and later confirmed. The lover, recovered from his first surprise and, accustomed to his happiness or guided by theory, which, always based on the most frequent cases, must only take light women into account—the lover, I say, demands more positive proofs and wishes to press his good fortune.

He is parried with indifference, coldness, even anger, if he show too much assurance—in France a shade of irony, which seems to say: "You are not quite as far as you think."

A woman behaves in this way, either because

she wakes up from a moment of intoxication, and obeys the word of modesty, which she trembles to have infringed, or simply through prudence or coquetry.

The lover comes to doubt of the happiness, to which he looked forward: he scans more narrowly the reasons that he fancied he had for hope.

He would like to fall back upon the other pleasures of life, and finds them annihilated. He is seized with the fear of a terrible disaster, and at the same time with a profound preoccupation.

7. Second crystallisation.

Here begins the second crystallisation, which forms diamonds out of the proofs of the idea—"She loves me."

The night which follows the birth of doubts, every quarter of an hour, after a moment of fearful unhappiness, the lover says to himself—"Yes, she loves me"—and crystallisation has its turn, discovering new charms. Then doubt with haggard eye grapples him and brings him to a standstill, blank. His heart forgets to beat—"But does she love me?" he says to himself. Between these alternatives, agonising and rapturous, the poor lover feels in his very soul: "She would give me pleasures, which she alone can give me and no one else."

It is the palpability of this truth, this path on the extreme edge of a terrible abyss and within touch, on the other hand, of perfect happiness, which gives so great a superiority to the second crystallisation over the first.

The lover wanders from moment to moment between these three ideas:—

1. She has every perfection.
2. She loves me.
3. What means of obtaining the greatest proof of her love?

The most agonising moment of love, still young, is when it sees the false reasoning it has made, and must destroy a whole span of crystallisation.

Doubt is the natural outcome of crystallisation.

CHAPTER IV

In a soul completely detached—a girl living in a lonely castle in the depth of the country—the slightest astonishment may bring on a slight admiration, and, if the faintest hope intervene, cause the birth of love and crystallisation (4).

In this case love delights, to begin with, just as a diversion.

Surprise and hope are strongly supported by

the need, felt at the age of sixteen, of love and sadness. It is well known that the restlessness of that age is a thirst for love, and a peculiarity of thirst is not to be extremely fastidious about the kind of draught that fortune offers.

Let us recapitulate the seven stages of love. They are:—

1. Admiration.
2. What pleasure, etc.
3. Hope.
4. Love is born.
5. First crystallisation.
6. Doubt appears.
7. Second crystallisation.

Between Nos. 1 and 2 may pass one year. One month between Nos. 2 and 3; but if hope does not make haste in coming, No. 2 is insensibly resigned as a source of unhappiness.

A twinkling of the eye between Nos. 3 and 4.

There is no interval between Nos. 4 and 5. The sequence can only be broken by intimate intercourse.

Some days may pass between Nos. 5 and 6, according to the degree to which the character is impetuous and used to risk, but between Nos. 6 and 7 there is no interval.

CHAPTER VIII

> *"This was her favoured fairy realm, and here she erected her aerial palaces."*
>
> —BRIDE OF LAMMERMOOR, CHAP. III.

A girl of eighteen has not enough crystallisation in her power, forms desires too limited by her narrow experiences of the things of life, to be in a position to love with as much passion as a woman of twenty-eight (4).

This evening I was exposing this doctrine to a clever woman, who maintains the contrary. "A girl's imagination being chilled by no disagreeable experience, and the prime of youth burning with all its force, any man can be the motive upon which she creates a ravishing image. Every time that she meets her lover, she will enjoy, not what he is in reality, but that image of delight which she has created for herself.

"Later, she is by this lover and by all men disillusioned, experience of the dark reality has lessened in her the power of crystallisation, mistrust has clipped the wings of imagination. At the instance of no man on earth, were he a very prodigy, could she form so irresistible an image: she could love no more with the same fire of her first youth. And as in love it is only the illusion formed by ourselves which we enjoy, never can the image, which she may create herself at twenty-eight, have the brilliance and the loftiness on which first love was built at sixteen: the second will always seem of a degenerate species."

"No, madam. Evidently it is the presence of mistrust, absent at sixteen, which must give to this second love a different colour. In early youth love is like an immense stream, which sweeps all before it in its course, and we feel that we cannot resist it. Now at twenty-eight a gentle heart knows itself: it knows that, if it is still to find some happiness in life, from love it must be claimed; and this poor, torn heart becomes the seat of a fearful struggle between love and mistrust. Crystallisation proceeds gradually; but the crystallisation, which emerges triumphant from this terrible proof, in which the soul in all its movements never loses sight of the most awful danger, is a thousand times more brilliant and more solid than crystallisation at sixteen, in which everything, by right of age, is gaiety and happiness."

"In this way love should be less gay and more passionate."

This conversation (Bologna, 9 March, 1820), bringing into doubt a point which seemed to me so clear, makes me believe more and more, that a man can say practically nothing with any sense on that which happens in the inmost heart of a woman of feeling: as to a coquet it is different—*we* also have senses and vanity.

The disparity between the birth of love in the two sexes would seem to come from the nature of their hopes, which are different. One attacks, the other defends; one asks, the other refuses; one is daring, the other timid.

The man reflects: "Can I please her? Will she love me?"

The woman: "When he says he loves me, isn't it for sport? Is his a solid character? Can he answer to himself for the length of his attachments?" Thus it is that many women regard and treat a young man of twenty-three as a child. If he has gone through six campaigns, he finds everything different—he is a young hero.

On the man's side, hope depends simply on the actions of that which he loves—nothing easier to interpret. On the side of woman, hope must rest on moral considerations—very difficult rightly to appreciate.

Most men demand such a proof of love, as to their mind dissipates all doubts; women are not so fortunate as to be able to find such a proof. And there is in life this trouble for lovers—that what makes the security and happiness of one, makes the danger and almost the humiliation of the other.

In love, men run the risk of the secret torture of the soul—women expose themselves to the scoffs of the public; they are more timid, and, besides, for them public opinion means much more.—"Sois considérée, il le faut."

They have not that sure means of ours of mastering public opinion by risking for an instant their life.

Women, then, must naturally be far more mistrustful. In virtue of their habits, all the mental movements, which form periods in the birth of love, are in their case more mild, more timid, more gradual and less decided. There is therefore a greater disposition to constancy; they will less easily withdraw from a crystallisation once begun.

A woman, seeing her lover, reflects with rapidity, or yields to the happiness of loving—happiness from which she is recalled in a disagreeable manner, if he make the least attack; for at the call to arms all pleasures must be abandoned.

The lover's part is simpler—he looks in the eyes of the woman he loves; a single smile can raise him to the zenith of happiness, and he looks continually for it. The length of the siege humiliates a man; on the contrary it makes a woman's glory.

A woman is capable of loving and, for an entire year, not saying more than ten or twelve words to the man whom she loves. At the bottom of her heart she keeps note how often she has seen him—twice she went with him to the theatre, twice she sat near him at dinner, three times he bowed to her out walking.

One evening during some game he kissed her hand: it is to be noticed that she allows no one since to kiss it under any pretext, at the risk even of seeming peculiar.

In a man, Léonore (6) remarked to me, such conduct would be called a feminine way of love.

CHAPTER IX

I make every possible effort to be dry. I would impose silence upon my heart, which feels that it has much to say. When I think that I have noted a truth, I always tremble lest I have written only a sigh.

CHAPTER X

In proof of crystallisation I shall content myself with recalling the following anecdote. A young woman hears that Edward, her relation, who is to return from the Army, is a youth of great distinction; she is assured that he loves her on her reputation; but he will want probably to see her, before making a proposal and asking her of her parents. She notices a young stranger at church, she hears him called Edward, she thinks of nothing but him—she is in love with him. Eight days later the real Edward arrives; he is not the Edward of church. She turns pale and will be unhappy for ever, if she is forced to marry him.

That is what the poor of understanding call an example of the senselessness of love.

A man of generosity lavishes the most delicate benefits upon a girl in distress. No one could have more virtues, and love was about to be born; but he wears a shabby hat, and she notices that he is awkward in the saddle. The girl confesses with a sigh that she cannot return the warm feelings, which he evidently has for her.

A man pays his attentions to a lady of the greatest respectability. She hears that this gentleman has had physical troubles of a comical nature: she finds him intolerable. And yet she had no intention of giving herself to him, and these secret troubles in no way blighted his understanding or amiability. It is simply that crystallisation was made impossible.

In order that a human being may delight in deifying an object to be loved, be it taken from the Ardennes forest or picked up at a Bal de Coulon, that it seems to him perfect is the first necessity—perfect by no means in every relation, but in every relation in which it is seen at the time. Perfect in all respects it will seem only after several days of the second crystallisation. The reason is simple—then it is enough to have the idea of a perfection in order to see it in the object of our love.

Beauty is only thus far necessary to the birth of love—ugliness must not form an obstacle. The lover soon comes to find his mistress beautiful, such as she is, without thinking of ideal beauty.

The features which make up the ideally beautiful would promise, if he could see them, a quantity of happiness, if I may use the expression, which

I would express by the number one; whereas the features of his mistress, such as they are, promise him one thousand units of happiness.

Before the birth of love beauty is necessary as advertisement: it predisposes us towards that passion by means of the praises, which we hear given to the object of our future love. Very eager admiration makes the smallest hope decisive.

In gallant-love, and perhaps in passion-love during the first five minutes, a woman, considering a possible lover, gives more weight to the way in which he is seen by other women, than to the way in which she sees him herself.

Hence the success of princes and officers. The pretty women of the Court of old king Lewis XIV were in love with that sovereign.

Great care should be taken not to offer facilities to hope, before it is certain that admiration is there. It might give rise to dullness, which makes love for ever impossible, and which, at any rate, is only to be cured by the sting of wounded pride.

No one feels sympathy for the simpleton, nor for a smile which is always there; hence the necessity in society of a veneer of rakishness—that is, the privileged manner. From too debased a plant we scorn to gather even a smile. In love, our vanity disdains a victory which is too easy; and in all matters man is not given to magnifying the value of an offering.

CHAPTER XII
FURTHER CONSIDERATION OF CRYSTALLISATION

Why do we enjoy with delight each new beauty, discovered in that which we love?

It is because each new beauty gives the full and entire satisfaction of a desire. You wish your mistress gentle—she is gentle; and then you wish her proud like Emilie in Corneille, and although these qualities are probably incompatible, instantly she appears with the soul of a Roman. That is the moral reason which makes love the strongest of the passions. In all others, desires must accommodate themselves to cold realities; here it is realities which model themselves spontaneously upon desires. Of all the passions, therefore, it is in love that violent desires find the greatest satisfaction.

There are certain general conditions of happiness, whose influence extends over every fulfilment of particular desires:—

1. She seems to belong to you, for you only can make her happy.

2. She is the judge of your worth. This condition was very important at the gallant and chivalrous Courts of Francis I and Henry II, and at the elegant Court of Lewis XV. Under a constitutional and rationalist government women lose this range of influence entirely.

3. For a romantic heart—The loftier her soul, the more sublime will be the pleasures that await her in your arms, and the more purified of the dross of all vulgar considerations.

The majority of young Frenchmen are, at eighteen, disciples of Rousseau; for them this condition of happiness is important.

In the midst of operations so apt to mislead our desire of happiness, there is no keeping cool.

For, the moment he is in love, the steadiest man sees no object such as it is. His own advantages he minimises, and magnifies the smallest favours of the loved one. Fears and hopes take at once a tinge of the romantic. (Wayward.) He no longer attributes anything to chance; he loses the perception of probability; in its effect upon his happiness a thing imagined is a thing existent.

A terrible symptom that you are losing your

head:—you think of some little thing which is difficult to make out; you see it white, and interpret that in favour of your love; a moment later you notice that actually it is black, and still you find it conclusively favourable to your love.

Then indeed the soul, a prey to mortal uncertainties, feels keenly the need of a friend. But there is no friend for the lover. The Court knew that; and it is the source of the only kind of indiscretion which a woman of delicacy might forgive.

CHAPTER XV

Suddenly in the midst of the most violent and the most thwarted passion come moments, when a man believes that he is in love no longer—as it were a spring of fresh water in the middle of the sea. To think of his mistress is no longer very much pleasure, and, although he is worn-out by the severity of her treatment, the fact that everything in life has lost its interest is a still greater misery. After a manner of existence which, fitful though it was, gave to all nature a new aspect, passionate and absorbing, now follows the dreariest and most despondent void.

It may be that your last visit to the woman,

whom you love, left you in a situation, from which, once before, your imagination had gathered the full harvest of sensation. For example, after a period of coldness, she has treated you less badly, letting you conceive exactly the same degree of hope and by the same external signs as on a previous occasion—all this perhaps unconsciously. Imagination picks up memory and its sinister warnings by the way, and instantly crystallisation ceases.

CHAPTER XVI

In a small port, the name of which I forget,
near Perpignan, 25th February, 1822.

This evening I have just found out that music, when it is perfect, puts the heart into the same state as it enjoys in the presence of the loved one—that is to say, it gives seemingly the keenest happiness existing on the face of the earth.

If this were so for all men, there would be no more favourable incentive to love.

But I had already remarked at Naples last year that perfect music, like perfect pantomime, makes me think of that which is at the moment the object of my dreams, and that the ideas, which it suggests to me, are excellent: at Naples, it was on the means of arming the Greeks.

Now this evening I cannot deceive myself—I have the misfortune *of being too great an admirer of milady L.*

And perhaps the perfect music, which I have had the luck to hear again, after two or three months of privation, although going nightly to the Opera, has simply had the effect, which I recognised long ago—I mean that of producing lively thoughts on what is already in the heart.

March 4th—eight days later.

I dare neither erase nor approve the preceding observation. Certain it is that, as I wrote it, I read it in my heart. If to-day I bring it into question, it is because I have lost the memory of what I saw at that time.

The habit of hearing music and dreaming its dreams disposes towards love. A sad and gentle air, provided it is not too dramatic, so that the imagination is forced to dwell on the action, is a direct stimulant to dreams of love and a delight for gentle and unhappy souls: for example, the drawn-out passage on the clarionet at the beginning of the quartet in *Bianca and Faliero* (10), and the recitative of La Camporesi towards the middle of the quartet.

A lover at peace with his mistress enjoys to distraction Rossini's famous duet in *Armida and Rinaldo*, depicting so justly the little doubts of happy love and the moments of delight which follow its reconciliations. It seems to him that the instrumental part, which comes in the middle of the duet, at the moment when Rinaldo wishes to fly, and represents in such an amazing way the conflict of the passions, has a physical influence upon his heart and touches it in reality. On this subject I dare not say what I feel; I should pass for a madman among people of the north.

CHAPTER XX

Perhaps men who are not susceptible to the feelings of passion-love are those most keenly sensitive to the effects of beauty: that at least is the strongest impression which such men can receive of women.

He who has felt his heart beating at a distant glimpse of the white satin hat of the woman he loves, is quite amazed by the chill left upon him by the approach of the greatest beauty in the world. He may even have a qualm of distress, to observe the excitement of others.

Extremely lovely women cause less surprise the

second day. 'Tis a great misfortune, it discourages crystallisation. Their merit being obvious to all and public property, they are bound to reckon more fools in the list of their lovers than princes, millionaires, etc.

CHAPTER XXI
LOVE AT FIRST SIGHT

Imaginative souls are sensitive and also mistrustful, even the most ingenuous,—I maintain. They may be suspicious without knowing it: they have had so many disappointments in life. Thus everything set-out and official, when a man is first introduced, scares the imagination and drives away the possibility of crystallisation; the romantic is then, on the contrary, love's triumph.

Nothing simpler—for in the supreme astonishment, which keeps the thoughts busy for long upon something out of the ordinary, is already half the mental exercise necessary to crystallisation.

I will quote the beginning of the Amours of Séraphine (*Gil Blas*, Bk. IV, Chap. X). It is Don Fernando who tells the story of his flight, when pursued by the agents of the inquisition . . .

After crossing several walks I came to a drawing-room, the door of which was also left open. I entered, and when I had observed all its magnificence . . . One side of the room a door stood ajar; I partly opened it and saw a suite of apartments whereof only the furthest was lighted. "What is to be done now?" I asked myself . . . I could not resist my curiosity . . . Advancing boldly, I went through all the rooms and reached one where there was a light—to wit, a taper upon a marble table in a silver-gilt candlestick . . . But soon afterwards, casting my eyes upon a bed, the curtains of which were partly drawn on account of the heat, I perceived an object which at once engrossed my attention: a young lady, fast asleep in spite of the noise of the thunder, which had just been bursting forth. I softly drew near her. My mind was suddenly troubled at the sight. Whilst I feasted my eyes with the pleasure of beholding her, she awoke.

Imagine her surprise at seeing in her room at midnight a man who was an utter stranger to her! She trembled on

> beholding me and shrieked aloud . . .
> I took pains to reassure her and
> throwing myself on my knees before her,
> said—"Madam, have no fear." She called
> her women . . . Grown a little braver
> by his (an old servant's) presence, she
> haughtily asked me who was, etc. etc.

There is an introduction not easily to be forgotten! On the other hand, could there be anything sillier in our customs of to-day than the official, and at the same time almost sentimental, introduction of the young wooer to his future wife: such legal prostitution goes so far as to be almost offensive to modesty.

"I have just been present this afternoon, February 17th, 1790," says Chamfort, "at a so-called family function. That is to say, men of respectable reputation and a decent company were congratulating on her good fortune Mlle. de Marille, a young person of beauty, wit and virtue, who is to be favoured with becoming the wife of M. R.—an unhealthy dotard, repulsive, dishonest, and mad, but rich: she has seen him for the third time to-day, when signing the contract. If anything characterises an age of infamy, it is the jubilation on an occasion like this, it is the folly of such joy and—looking ahead—the sanctimonious cruelty, with which the same society will heap contempt without reserve upon the pettiest imprudence of a poor young woman in love."

Ceremony of all kinds, being in its essence something affected and set-out beforehand, in which the point is to act "properly," paralyses the imagination and leaves it awake only to that which is opposed to the object of the ceremony, e.g. something comical—whence the magic effect of the slightest joke. A poor girl, struggling against nervousness and attacks of modesty during the official introduction of her *fiancé*, can think of nothing but the part she is playing, and this again is a certain means of stifling the imagination.

Modesty has far more to say against getting into bed with a man whom you have seen but twice, after three Latin words have been spoken in church, than against giving way despite yourself to the man whom for two years you have adored. But I am talking double Dutch.

The fruitful source of the vices and mishaps, which follow our marriages nowadays, is the Church of Rome. It makes liberty for girls impossible before marriage, and divorce impossible, when once they have made their mistake, or rather when they find out the mistake of the choice forced on them. Compare Germany, the land of happy marriages: a delightful princess (Madame la Duchesse de Sa——) has just married in all good faith for the fourth time, and has not failed to ask to the wedding her three first husbands, with whom she is on the best terms. That is going too far; but a single divorce, which punishes a husband for his tyranny, prevents a thousand cases of unhappy wedded life. What is amusing is that Rome is one of the places where you see most divorces.

Love goes out at first sight towards a face, which reveals in a man at once something to respect and something to pity.

CHAPTER XXII
OF INFATUATION

The most fastidious spirits are very given to curiosity and prepossession: this is to be seen, especially, in beings in which that sacred fire, the source of the passions, is extinct—in fact it is one of the most fatal symptoms. There is also the infatuation of schoolboys just admitted to society. At the two poles of life, with too much or too little sensibility, there is little chance of simple people getting the right effect from things, or feeling the genuine sensation which they ought to give. These beings, either too ardent or excessive in their ardour, amorous on credit, if one may use the expression, throw themselves at objects instead of awaiting them.

From afar off and without looking they enfold things in that imaginary charm, of which they find a perennial source within themselves, long before sensation, which is the consequence of the object's nature, has had time to reach them. Then, on coming to close quarters, they see these things not such as they are, but as they have made them; they think they are enjoying such and such an object, while, under cover of that object, they are enjoying themselves. But one fine day a man gets tired of keeping the whole thing going; he discovers that his idol is *not playing the game*; infatuation collapses and the resulting shock to his self-esteem makes him unfair to that which he appreciated too highly.

JEROME K. JEROME

On Being in Love

You've been in love, of course! If not you've got it to come. Love is like the measles; we all have to go through it. Also, like the measles, we take it only once. One need never be afraid of catching it a second time. The man who has had it can go into the most dangerous places, and play the most fool-hardy tricks with perfect safety. He can picnic in shady woods, ramble through leafy aisles, and linger on mossy seats to watch the sunset. He fears a quiet country house no more than he would his own club. He can join a family party to go down the Rhine. He can, to see the last of a friend, venture into the very jaws of the marriage ceremony itself. He can keep his head through the whirl of a ravishing waltz, and rest afterward in a dark conservatory, catching nothing more lasting than a cold. He can brave a moonlight walk adown sweet-scented lanes, or a twilight pull among the somber rushes. He can get over a stile without danger, scramble through a tangled hedge without being caught, come down a slippery path without falling. He can look into sunny eyes, and not be dazzled. He listens to the siren voices, yet sails on with unveered helm. He clasps white hands in his, but no electric "Lulu"-like force holds him bound in their dainty pressure.

No, we never sicken with love twice. Cupid spends no second arrow on the same heart. Love's handmaids are our lifelong friends. Respect, and Admiration, and Affection, our doors may always be left open for, but their great celestial master, in his royal progress, pays but one visit, and departs. We like, we cherish, we are very, very fond of—but we never love again. A man's heart is a fire-work that once in its time flashes heavenward. Meteor-like it blazes for a moment, and lights with its glory the whole world beneath. Then the night of our sordid common-place life closes in around it, and the burned-out case, falling back to earth, lies useless and uncared for, slowly smoldering into ashes. Once, breaking loose from our prison bonds, we dare, as mighty old Prometheus dared, to scale the Olympian mount, and snatch from Phœbus's chariot the fire of the gods. Happy those who, hastening down again ere it dies out, can kindle their earthly altars at its flame. Love is too pure a light to burn long among the noisome gases that we breathe, but before it is choked out we may use it as a torch to ignite the cosy fire of affection.

And, after all, that warming glow is more suited to our cold little back parlor of a world than is the burning spirit, love. Love should be the vestal fire of some mighty temple—some vast, dim fane whose organ music is the rolling of the spheres. Affection will burn cheerily when the white flame of love is flickered out. Affection is a fire that can be fed from day to day, and be piled up ever higher as the wintery years draw nigh. Old men and women can sit by it with their thin hands clasped, the little children can nestle down in front, the friend and neighbor has his welcome corner by its side, and even shaggy Fido and sleek Titty can toast their noses at the bars.

Let us heap the coals of kindness upon that fire. Throw on your pleasant words, your gentle pressures of the hand, your thoughtful and unselfish deeds. Fan it with good humor, patience, and forbearance. You can let the wind blow and the rain fall unheeded then, for your hearth will be warm and bright, and the faces round it will make sunshine in spite of the clouds without.

I am afraid, dear Edwin and Angelina, you expect too much from love. You think there is enough of your little hearts to feed this fierce, devouring passion for all your long lives. Ah, young folk! don't rely too much upon that unsteady flicker. It will dwindle and dwindle as the months roll on, and there is no replenishing the fuel. You will watch it die out in anger and disappointment. To each it will seem that it is the other who is growing colder. Edwin sees with bitterness that Angelina no longer runs to the gate to meet him, all smiles and blushes; and when he has a cough now, she doesn't begin to cry, and, putting her arms round his neck say that she can not live without him. The most she will probably do is to suggest a lozenge, and even that in a tone implying that it is the noise more than anything else she is anxious to get rid of.

Poor little Angelina, too, sheds silent tears, for Edwin has given up carrying her old handkerchief in the inside pocket of his waistcoat.

Both are astonished at the falling off in the other one, but neither sees their own change. If they did, they would not suffer as they do. They would look for the cause in the right quarter—in the littleness of poor human nature—join hands over their common failing, and start building their house anew on a more earthly and enduring foundation. But we are so blind to our own shortcomings, so wide awake to those of others. Everything that happens to us is always the other person's fault. Angelina would have gone on loving Edwin for ever and ever and ever, if only Edwin had not grown so strange and different. Edwin would have adored Angelina through eternity, if Angelina had only remained the same as when he first adored her.

It is a cheerless hour for you both, when the lamp of love has gone out, and the fire of affection is not yet lighted, and you have to grope about in the cold raw dawn of life to kindle it. God grant it catches light before the day is too far spent. Many sit shivering by the dead coals till night come.

But, there! of what use is it to preach? Who that feels the rush of young love through his veins can think it will ever flow feeble and slow? To the boy of twenty it seems impossible that he will not love as wildly at sixty as he does then. He can not call to mind any middle-aged or elderly gentleman of his acquaintance who is known to exhibit symptoms of frantic attachment, but that does not interfere in his belief in himself. His love will never fail, whoever else's may. Nobody ever loved as he loves, and so, of course, the rest of the world's experience can be no guide in his case. Alas, alas! ere thirty he has joined the ranks of the sneerers. It is not his fault. Our passions, both the good and bad, cease with our blushes. We do not hate, nor grieve, nor joy, nor despair in our thirties like we did in our teens. Disappointment does not suggest suicide, and we quaff success without intoxication.

We take all things in a minor key as we grow older. There are few majestic passages in the latter acts of life's opera. Ambition takes a less ambitious aim. Honor becomes more reasonable and conveniently adapts itself to circumstances. And love—love dies. "Irreverence for the dreams of youth" soon creeps like a killing frost upon our hearts. The tender shoots and the expanding flowers are nipped and withered, and of a vine that yearned to stretch its tendrils round the world, there is left but a sapless stump.

My fair friends will deem all this rank heresy, I know. So far from a man's not loving after he has passed boyhood, it is not till there is a good deal of gray in his hair that they think his protestations at all worthy of attention. Young ladies take their notions of our sex from the novels written by their own, and compared with the monstrosities that masquerade for men in the pages of that nightmare literature, Pythagoras's plucked bird and Frankenstein's demon were fair average specimens of humanity.

In these so-called books, the chief lover, or Greek god, as he is admiringly referred to—by the way, they do not say which "Greek god" it is that the gentleman bears such a striking likeness to, it might be hump-backed Vulcan, or double-faced Janus, or even driveling Silenus, the god of abstruse mysteries. He resembles the whole family of them, however, in being a blackguard, and perhaps this is what is meant. To even the little manliness his classical prototypes possessed, though, he can lay no claim whatever, being a listless, effeminate noodle, on the shady side of forty. But oh! the depth and strength of this elderly party's emotion for some bread-and-butter school-girl! Hide your heads, ye young Romeos and Leanders, this *blasé* old beau loves with an hysterical fervor that requires four adjectives to every noun to properly describe.

It is well, dear ladies, for us old sinners, that you study only books. Did you read mankind, you would know that the lad's shy stammering tells a truer tale than our bold eloquence. A boy's love comes from a full heart; a man's is more often the result of a full stomach. Indeed, a man's sluggish current may not be called love, compared with the rushing fountain that wells up when a boy's heart is struck with the heavenly rod. If you would taste love, drink of the pure stream that youth pours out at your feet. Do not wait till it has become a muddy river before you stoop to catch its waves.

Or is it that you like its bitter flavor; that the clear, limpid water is insipid to your palate, and that the pollution of its after-course gives it a relish to your lips? Must we believe those who tell us that a hand foul with the filth of a shameful life is the only one a young girl cares to be caressed by?

That is the teaching that is bawled out day by day from between those yellow covers. Do they ever pause to think, I wonder, those devil's lady-helps, what mischief they are doing crawling about God's garden, and telling childish Eves and silly Adams that sin is sweet, and that decency is ridiculous and vulgar? How many an innocent girl do they not degrade into an evil-minded woman? To how many a weak lad do they not point out the dirty by-path as the shortest cut to a maiden's heart? It is not as if they wrote of life as it really is. Speak truth, and right will take care of itself. But their pictures are coarse daubs painted from the sickly fancies of their own diseased imaginations.

We want to think of women not—as their own sex would show them—as Loreleis luring us to destruction, but as good angels beckoning us upward. They have more power for good or evil than they dream of. It is just at the very age when a man's character is forming that he tumbles into love, and then the lass he loves has the making or marring of him. Unconsciously he molds himself to what she would have him, good or bad. I am sorry to have to be ungallant enough to say that I do not think they always use their influence for the best. Too often the female world is bounded hard and fast within the limits of the commonplace. Their ideal hero is a prince of littleness, and to become that many a powerful mind, enchanted by love, is "lost to life and use, and name and fame."

And yet, women, you could make us so much better, if you only would. It rests with you more than with all the preachers, to roll this world a little nearer heaven. Chivalry is not dead; it only sleeps for want of work to do. It is you who must wake it to noble deeds. You must be worthy of knightly worship. You must be higher than ourselves. It was for Una that the Red Cross Knight did war. For no painted, mincing Court dame could the dragon have been slain. Oh, ladies fair, be fair in mind and soul as well as face, so that brave knights may win glory in your service! Oh, woman, throw off your disguising cloaks of selfishness, effrontery, and affectation! Stand forth once more a queen in your royal robe of simple purity. A thousand swords, now rusting in ignoble sloth, shall leap from their scabbards to do battle for your honor against wrong. A thousand Sir Rolands shall lay lance in rest, and Fear, Avarice, Pleasure, and Ambition shall go down in the dust before your colors.

What noble deeds were we not ripe for in the days when we loved? What noble lives could we not have lived for her sake? Our love was a religion we could have died for. It was no mere human creature like ourselves that we adored. It was a queen that we paid homage to, a goddess that we worshipped.

And how madly we did worship! And how sweet it was to worship! Ah, lad, cherish love's young dream while it lasts! You will know, too soon, how truly little Tom Moore sung when he said that there was nothing half so sweet in life. Even when it brings misery, it is a wild, romantic misery, all unlike the dull, worldly pain of after sorrows. When you have lost her—when the light is gone out from your life, and the world stretches before you a long, dark horror, even then a half enchantment mingles with your despair.

And who would not risk its terrors to gain its raptures? Ah, what raptures they were! The mere recollection thrills you. How delicious it was to tell her that you loved her, that you lived for her, that you would die for her! How you did rave, to be sure; what floods of extravagant nonsense you poured forth, and oh, how cruel it was of her to pretend not to believe you! In what awe you stood of her! How miserable you were when you had offended her! And yet, how pleasant to be bullied by her, and to sue for pardon without having the slightest notion of what your fault was! How dark the world was when she snubbed you, as she often did, the little rogue, just to see you look wretched; how sunny when she smiled! How jealous you were of every one about her! How you hated every man she shook hands with, every woman she kissed—the maid that did her hair, the boy that cleaned her shoes, the dog she nursed—though you had to be respectful to the last named! How you looked forward to seeing her, how stupid you were when you did see her, staring at her without saying a word! How impossible it was for you to go out at any time of the day or night without finding yourself eventually opposite her windows! You hadn't pluck enough to go in, but you hung about the corner and gazed at the outside. Oh, if the house had only caught fire—it was insured, so it wouldn't have mattered—and you could have rushed in and saved her at the risk of your life, and have been terribly burned and injured! Anything to serve her. Even in little things that was so sweet. How you would watch her, spaniel-like, to anticipate her slightest wish! How proud you were to do her bidding! How delightful it was to be ordered about by her! To devote your whole life to her, and to never think of yourself, seemed such a simple thing. You would go without a holiday to lay an humble offering at her shrine, and felt more than repaid if she only deigned to accept it. How precious to you was everything that she had hallowed by her touch—her little glove, the ribbon she had worn, the rose that had nestled in her hair, and whose withered leaves still mark the poems you never care to look at now!

And oh, how beautiful she was, how wondrous

beautiful! It was as some angel entering the room, and all else became plain and earthly. She was too sacred to be touched. It seemed almost presumption to gaze at her. You would as soon have thought of kissing her as of singing comic songs in a cathedral. It was desecration enough to kneel and timidly raise the gracious little hand to your lips.

Ah, those foolish days, those foolish days, when we were unselfish and pure-minded; those foolish days, when our simple hearts were full of truth, and faith, and reverence! Ah, those foolish days of noble longings and of noble strivings! And oh, these wise, clever days, when we know that money is the only prize worth striving for, when we believe in nothing else but meanness and lies, when we care for no living creature but ourselves!

MAE M. FRANKING

My Chinese Marriage

I saw Chan-King Liang for the first time on a certain Monday morning in October. It was the opening day of college, and the preceding week had been filled with the excitement incidental to the arrival of many students in a small town given over to family life. Every household possessed of a spare room was impressed with the fact that good citizenship demanded that it harbor a student. Therefore, when I saw trunks and boxes and bags being tumbled upon the front porch of our next-door neighbor, I said to Mother, "Mrs. James has succumbed!" and set out for my first class with Celia, an old friend.

As we crossed the campus, we noticed a group of boys, gathered on the steps of College Hall and talking among themselves. Celia turned to me. "Do you see the one with very black hair, his face turned away a little—the one in the gray suit, Margaret?—Well, that is the new Chinese student, and the boys all say he is a wonder. My cousin knew him last year in Chicago, where he was a freshman. Going in for international law and political science—imagine!"

I turned and glanced with a faint interest at the foreign student, on whose black hair the sun was shining. My first impression was of a very young, smiling lad. "Looks well enough," I said, rather ungraciously, and we passed on.

I was a busy student, eagerly beginning my freshman year's work, and I thought no more of the young Chinese. But a day or so later I discovered him to be the owner of those trunks and bags I had seen assembled on Mrs. James's porch. Chan-King was my next-door neighbor.

We were never introduced to each other, as it happened, and, though we shared studies in German and French, we did not exchange a word for some time. Later I found myself admiring his feat of learning two foreign languages through the medium of English, a third, and doing it so very well. At the same time, though I was not then aware of the fact, he was also admiring me for proficiency in these subjects, in which I was working hard, because I intended to teach languages.

The progress of my interest in him was

gradual and founded on a sense of his complete remoteness, an utter failure to regard him as a human being like the rest of us. He was the first of his race I had ever seen. But finally we spoke to one another by some chance, and, after that, it seemed unnecessary to refuse to walk to class with him on a certain morning when we came out of our houses at the same moment.

We parted at College Hall door with an exchange of informal little nods. I was happily impressed, but my impulse to friendship suffered a quick reaction from all that Chan-King was, when viewed against the background of his race as I saw it. I had no intention whatever of continuing our association.

Naturally, Chan-King knew nothing of this. I think I was probably a trifle more courteous to him than was necessary. I remember being uneasy for fear of wounding him by some thoughtless remark that would reveal my true state of mind about China. I lost sight of the race in the individual. I even pretended not to notice that he was waiting for me morning after morning when I emerged, always a trifle late, hurrying to classes. By the close of the first semester, we were making the trip together almost daily as a matter of course.

He was gay and friendly, with a sort of frank joyousness that was his own special endowment for living. I enjoyed his companionship, his talk, his splendid spirit. His cheerfulness was a continual stimulant to my moody, introspective, static temperament. I used to study his face, which in repose had the true oriental impassivity—a stillness that suggested an inner silence or brooding. But this mood was rare in those days, and I remember best his laughter, his shining eyes that never missed the merriment to be had from the day's routine events.

For a while we were merely two very conventional young students walking sedately together, talking with eagerness on what now seem amusingly sober and carefully chosen subjects. We were both determined to be dignified and impersonal. I was nineteen, and Chan-King was two years older.

Finally, Chan-King asked to call and he appeared at the door that evening, laden with an enormous, irregular package, a collection of treasures that he thought might interest us. We all gathered about the library table, where he spread a flaming array of embroidered silks, carved ivory and sandalwood and curious little images in bronze and blackwood. They gave out a delicious fragrance, spicy and warm and sweet, with a bitter tang to it, a mingling of oils and lacquers and dust of incense.

He was very proud of half a dozen neckties his mother had made him, patterned carefully after the American one he had sent her as a souvenir. "She sews a great deal, and everything she does is beautiful," he said, stroking one of the ties, fashioned of wine-colored silk and embroidered in a thin gold thread.

The simple words, the tangle of the exotic things lying on the table, in that moment set the whole world between us. I saw him as alien, far removed and unknowable; I realized how utterly transplanted he must be, moving as he did in a country whose ideals, manners and customs must appear, at times, grotesquely fantastic to him. "How queer we must seem to you!" I exclaimed, impulsively, lifting a solid, fat little idol in my hand.

"Queer? Not at all—but wonderfully interesting in everything. You see, to me it is all one world!" Our eyes met for a second. Then he offered me a small embroidered Chinese flag. I hesitated, looking at the writhing, fire-breathing dragon done in many-colored silks. Again the old prejudice swept over me. I was about to refuse.

But I saw in his eyes an expression of hesitating, half-anxious pleading, which touched me. I took the flag, puzzled a trifle over that look I had surprised.

Chan-King became a frequent visitor at our home in the evenings, making friends with my father and mother, with true Chinese deference. I like to remember those times, with all of us sitting around the big table, the shaded lamp casting a clear circle of light on the books and papers, the rest of the room in pleasant dimness. It was during these evenings that Chan-King told us about his father, typical Chinese product of his clan and time, who had early perceived the limitations of a too nationalistic point of view and had planned western education for his sons, of whom Chan-King was the eldest. From his talk I reconstructed a half-picture of his home in southern China. It was a large household of brothers and relatives and servants ruled over by his mother during the prolonged absences of his father, whose business interests lay in a faraway island port.

Once he brought a faded photograph of a small boy formally arrayed in the Chinese velvets and satins of an earlier period. "Myself at the age of six," he explained.

I examined the picture closely. "Why, Mr. Liang," I said, in wonder, "you are wearing a—wearing a—queue!"

He smiled, delighted at my confusion. "Yes, a very nice queue it was," he declared, "bound with a scarlet silk cord. I remember how it waved in the wind when I flew my kite on the hills!"

"You wore a black queue yourself, Margaret," interposed my mother, her eyes twinkling, "shorter than this, but often tied with a red silk ribbon."

"You see, we had that in common, at least," said Chan-King. And he flashed a grateful smile at mother. There was a well-established friendship between my kindly, understanding mother and Chan-King while my feeling for him was still uncertain.

Yet in spite of all these reasons for close sympathy with Chan-King, I felt toward him at times something amounting almost to dislike. Against such states of mind my sense of personal justice, a trait I had directly from my Scotch inheritance, instantly rebelled. I was careful in no way to reveal my feelings, though I probably should have done so had I even remotely realized that friendship was verging upon love. As it was, I had an ideal of genuine comradeship, of a pleasant interlude destined to end with our college days.

Toward the end of the winter, as our acquaintance advanced, there came to me a series of those revulsions. I assured myself that so ephemeral a relation as ours must be was hardly worth the time I was giving to it. I remembered that, fine as Chan-King was, he belonged to the Chinese race. I decided to put an end to the entire episode at once. The way in which I carried out this plan was unnecessarily abrupt. I avoided him, unmistakably, going to class and returning home by a roundabout way, and refusing to see him either in class or on the campus.

Then, one afternoon at the end of two weeks, he was waiting for me before the main door of College Hall. I did not speak. He joined me without a word and walked in silence to the campus edge. I turned suddenly toward a side street. "Go that way if you like," I said, rudely. "I have an errand this way."

He came with me. "I wish to talk with you," he said, with an oddly restrained, patient tone of weariness. Our eyes met, and I saw in his a gentle and touching determination to understand and be understood, which would have been more significant to me if I had been less engrossed in my own emotions.

"Why do you wish to end our friendship?" he asked, quietly, with his characteristic frankness.

"I—because I thought it was best," I stammered, completely disarmed.

"It is never best to give up a friendship," he said. "But it happens that our friendship may end soon after all. It is possible I shall return to China. To-day I received a cablegram from my father, saying my mother is dangerously ill. I shall know within a day or so whether I am to go or to stay."

Human sympathy triumphed over race prejudice. "Come home with me," I said, "and let mother talk to you. She always knows what to say."

Another cablegram two days later brought the good news of his mother's improvement. Chan-King's anxiety during those two days wrung me. He said nothing, but his face was strained and lined. He walked and we talked a good deal of other things, and he gave me definite outlines of his "life-plan," as he called it. He regarded the diplomatic service of his country as his final goal, but, on the way to it, he wished to take part in constructive teaching and sociological work in China. He was keenly enthusiastic about the ancient arts and natural beauties of China and venerated many of her old customs. "I hope introducing modern education will not destroy the beauty of the East," he told me, but he was solidly convinced of the need for new ideas in all the Orient. I began to see his country through new eyes.

We were soon going about together a great deal. I remember many happy parties on the lantern-lighted campus, many field-days and tennis matches, all the innocent freedom of college life that we enjoyed together. I was rather remote in my personal friendships, and very little was said to me regarding my association with the Chinese student. But now I began to hear small murmurs, a vague hum of discussion, and to observe an interested watching of us by the students and townspeople. I could not help seeing that curious glances followed us when we entered a tea-room or concert hall together.

Several friends of my mother's spoke disapprovingly to her of the matter. "What if they should fall in love—marry?" asked one conventional-minded old lady. But my mother was born without prejudices and never sees boundary lines or nationalities. She was infinitely tactful and kind. I know now that she was rather uneasy, for she felt that marriage is a difficult enough relation when each person knows the other's heritage and formulas; but she said nothing to make me self-conscious, not even repeating the remarks of her acquaintances until long afterward.

However, I heard comments from other sources, which irritated me a trifle and had the perfectly natural effect of stimulating my loyalty to Chan-King and arousing at times a yearning tenderness to shield him from injustice. At this time we tentatively expressed our views on intermarriage. We were sitting on the porch late one afternoon. "I believe marriage between alien races is a mistake," I said, in the decisive way I cultivated at that time. "It is better to marry one's own kind."

"No doubt there are fewer difficulties," he answered, without conviction. "It is all so much a personal problem. Marriages between Americans do not seem to be always successful."

I flared. "We hear only of the unhappy ones," I retorted.

"But there are many, many unhappy ones, then," he returned gently. "I wonder if unhappy marriage in all countries is not due to selfishness and lack of love and to unwillingness to compromise on unimportant differences."

We could not possibly quarrel here, and our talk proceeded amiably.

My thoughts at dinner that night seem very amusing to me as I recall them now. Chan-King was so like one of us, as we sat at table together, that I found myself wondering if it was true that a Chinese wife did not eat at the same table with her husband; if she actually did wait upon him and obey him without question in everything; if Chan-King would return to China soon and there become an insufferable, autocratic eastern husband. The thought oppressed me unbearably. Since Chan-King was leaving next day on a summer-vacation trip, this was a farewell dinner. He insisted on helping me with the dishes afterward, for ours was a simple household, and we usually had no maid. We were very merry over the task. "In China," he confided, as he stacked the saucers, "the lot of women is much easier. They have servants for everything of this kind. I know an Englishwoman who married a Chinese, and she afterward taught in a college for the sake of something to do."

"She did quite right," I said. "Idleness is not good for any one."

"Chinese wives are not idle," he answered, gravely; "they have many duties for everyone in their household."

At this he turned his eyes upon me, with an intent, inner look. Because I was impressed, I chose to be flippant.

"If I obstruct your view, I will move," I said.

"It would do no good," he answered. "You are always there—wherever I want to look."

Later he was writing his name in Chinese characters on a photograph he had given my mother. I stood beside him. He dropped the pen, turned to me and took both my hands in his own. He bent toward me, and I drew away, shaking my head decisively. I wrenched one hand free, and the kiss he meant for my lips reached my fingers instead. I was overwhelmed with a sense of invasion. We quarreled, but without bitterness or real anger. I was simply convinced that, since love was not for us, we were bound by all ethics to keep our relations in the outward seeming of friendship. For a moment I felt that one of my ideals had been rudely shattered.

"Oh, but you have mistaken me!" he declared, earnestly, refusing to release my hand.

"Kisses are not for friendship," I managed to say.

"I'm sorry," he confessed, but I saw in his eyes that he regretted my misunderstanding of him, nothing more.

During his summer travels he wrote me many letters. I had time to think, and in my thoughts I admitted that to be a friend to Chan-King was better than to have the love of any one else in the world.

When he returned, we wandered together one evening down to the campus and sat on a stone bench in the moon-shade of a tall tree. I had overheard a remark, tinged with race prejudice, that had awakened again in my heart that brooding maternal tenderness, and when Chan-King's eyes pleaded wistfully, I gave him, as a sacrificial offering, the kiss before denied.

That fall he transferred for a year to a New England university. He told me long afterward it was so that absence might teach me to know my own heart. I loved him now and admitted it to myself with bitter honesty. But all fulfilment of love seemed so hopeless and remote, the chasm fixed between our races seemed so impassable, that I gave up in my heart and put away his letters as they came, smiling with affected youthful cynicism at the memory of that kiss, which could mean nothing more to us than a sweet and troubled recollection.

He came back unexpectedly at the end of the college term. There was an indescribably hopeful, anxious look in his eyes as he took my hands. My first sight of his face, grown older and graver in those long months, brought a shock of poignant happiness, very near to tears. Off guard, we met as lovers, with all antagonisms momentarily swept away, all pretenses forgotten. I went to his arms as my one sure haven. For this hour love made everything simple and happy.

My father and mother were astonished when we told them of our intention to marry. With gentle wisdom, mother suggested that we allow ourselves a year of engagement, "in order to be sure," as she expressed it. We were very sure but we consented.

Chan-King wrote at once to his people in south China, telling of his engagement. For me, he had one important explanation, made in his frank, straightforward way. "In China," he told me, "it is usual for parents to arrange their children's marriages, often years in advance. When I was very young, it was generally understood that I would later marry the daughter of my father's good friend, three years younger than I. There was no formal betrothal, and, when I left home to study, I asked my father not to make any definite plans for my marriage until my return. The subject has never been mentioned since, and I don't know what his ideas are now. But they can make no difference with us—you understand that, Margaret, dear?" Again I felt myself in spiritual collision with unknown forces and wondered at his calmness in opposing the claims of his heredity.

His family replied to his letter with a cable gram, forbidding the marriage. I had never seriously expected any other decision. A letter followed, conciliatory in tone, in which his father explained that since Chan-King's foreign education was nearly completed, arrangements had been made for his marriage to Miss Li-Ying immediately upon his return home. He gave a charming description of his bride, whom Chan-King had not seen for twelve years. She was, he said, young and modest and kind, she was beautiful and wealthy, and moreover had been given a modern education in order to fit her for the position of wife to an advanced Chinese. The match was greatly desired by both families. In conclusion, the letter urgently requested that Chan-King would not make it impossible for his father to fulfil the contract he had entered into with a friend, and very gently intimated that by so doing he would forfeit all right to further consideration.

There were other letters. An American friend, a missionary, wrote—oh, very tactfully—of the difficulties he would have in keeping an American wife happy in the Orient. A Chinese cousin discussed at length the sorrows a foreign daughter-in-law would bring into his house—the bitterness of having in the family an alien and stubborn woman, who would be unwilling to give his parents the honor due them or to render them the service they would expect of their son's wife.

Many letters of this kind came in a group. There was a hopeless tone of finality, a solid clan consciousness in those letters that frightened me a little. I was uneasy, uncertain. I had found no irreconcilable elements in our minds, for I was very conservative West, and he was very liberal East. But here were represented the people with whom his life must be spent and the social background against which it must harmoniously unfold. I felt with terrific force that it was not Chan-King, but Chan-King's traditions and ancestors, his tremendous racial past, that I must reckon with.

Also, I did not wish to stand in the way of his future. I doubt if I could have found courage to marry Chan-King, if I had then realized the importance—especially in diplomatic and political circles—of clan and family influence in China. But he gave it up so freely, with such assured and unregretful cheerfulness, that I could not but share his mood.

In these calm, logical, impersonal family letters, which Chan-King translated for me, there was a strain of sinister philosophy that chilled me as I read. The letters dealt entirely with his duty in its many phases—to his parents, to his ancestors, to his country, to his own future. Nothing of love! Only one relative—a cousin—mentioned it at all, and in this wise: "You are young now, and to youth love seems of great importance. But as age replaces youth, you will find that love runs away like water."

"That is not true, Chan-King," I said, with solemn conviction. "Love is greater than life or age; it lives beyond death. It is love that makes eternity!"

At this time, Chan-King did not quite comprehend my mystical interpretation of love. But he answered very happily, "To have you for my wife is worth everything else the world can offer."

Chan-King continued to write to his family briefly and respectfully, declining to be influenced in any way. Replies came at lengthening intervals and then ceased. There was no open breach, no violent tearing asunder of bonds. Courteously, quite gently, the hands of his people were removed, and he stood alone.

"But surely your mother will not give you up!" I exclaimed one day when it dawned on me that not one message had she sent in all the correspondence.

"Not in her dear heart," he said, with unshaken faith, "but of course she will not write to me if my father disapproves."

"But a mother, Chan-King!" I protested. "Surely her feelings come first always!"

Chan-King's tone was patient after the manner of one who has explained an obvious fact many times. "In China," he reminded me again, "the family comes always before the individual. But with you and me, Margaret beloved, love has first importance."

RAINER MARIA RILKE

To Friedrich Westhoff

Villa Strohl-Fern, Rome
April 29, 1904

Through Mother we have heard of you often lately, and without knowing anything more specific about you, we nevertheless feel that you are having a hard time. Mother will not be able to help you, for at bottom no one in life can help anyone else in life; this one experiences over and over in every conflict and every perplexity: that one is alone.

That isn't as bad as it may at first glance appear; and again it is the best thing in life that each should have everything in himself: his fate, his future, his whole expanse and world. There are moments, to be sure, when it is difficult to be in oneself and to persist within one's own ego; it happens that at the very instants when one should hold faster and—one would almost have to say—more obstinately than ever to oneself, one attaches oneself to something external, during important events transfers one's own center out of oneself into something alien, into another person. That goes against the very simplest laws of equilibrium, and only difficulty can come of it.

Clara and I, dear Friedrich, have found ourselves and come to an understanding in the very fact that all companionship can consist only in the strengthening of two neighboring solitudes, whereas everything that one is wont to call giving oneself is by nature harmful to companionship: for when a person abandons himself, he is no longer anything, and when two people both give themselves up in order to come close to each other, there is no longer any ground beneath them and their being together is a continual falling.—We have learned such things, my dear Friedrich, not without great pain, have learned what everyone who wants his own life gets to know somehow or other.

Sometime when I am older and more mature I shall perhaps get around to writing a book, a book for young people; not by any means because I think I have been able to do anything better than others. On the contrary, because from childhood on and during my entire youth everything became so much more difficult for me than for other young people.

So I learned over and over again that there is scarcely anything more difficult than to love one another. That it is work, day labor, Friedrich, day labor; God knows there is no other word for it. And look, added to this is the fact that young people are not prepared for such difficult loving; for convention has tried to make this most complicated and ultimate relationship into something easy and frivolous, has given it the appearance of everyone's being able to do it. It is not so. Love is something difficult and it is more difficult than other things because in other conflicts Nature herself enjoins men to collect themselves, to take themselves firmly in hand with all their strength, while in the heightening of love the impulse is to give oneself wholly away. But just think, can that be anything beautiful, to give oneself away not as something whole and ordered, but haphazard rather, bit by bit, as it comes? Can such giving away, that looks so like a throwing away and dismemberment, be anything good, can it be happiness, joy, progress? No, it cannot . . . When you give someone flowers, you arrange them beforehand, don't you? But young people who love each other fling themselves to each other in the impatience and haste of their passion, and they don't notice at all what a lack of mutual esteem lies in this disordered giving of themselves, they notice it with astonishment and indignation only from the dissension that arises between them out of all this disorder. And once there is disunity between them, the confusion grows with every day; neither of the two has anything unbroken, pure, and unspoiled about him any longer, and amid the disconsolateness of a break they try to hold fast to the semblance of their happiness (for all that was really supposed to be for the sake of happiness). Alas, they are scarcely able to recall any more what they meant by happiness. In his uncertainty each becomes more and more unjust toward the other; they who wanted to do each other good are now handling one another in an imperious and intolerant manner, and in the struggle somehow to get out of their untenable and unbearable state of confusion, they commit the greatest fault that can happen to human relationships: they become impatient. They hurry to a conclusion, to come, as they believe, to a final decision, they try once and for all to establish their relationship, whose surprising changes have frightened them, in order to remain the same now and *forever* (as they say). That is only the last error in this long chain of errings linked fast to one another. What is dead cannot even be clung to (for it crumbles and changes its character); how much less can what is living and alive be treated definitively, once and for all. Self-transformation is precisely what life is, and human relationships, which are an extract of life, are the most changeable of all, rising and falling from minute to minute, and lovers are those in whose relationship and contact no one moment resembles another. People between whom nothing accustomed, nothing that has already been present before ever takes place, but many new, unexpected, unprecedented things. There are such relationships which must be a very great, almost unbearable happiness, but they can occur only between very rich natures and between those who, each for himself, are richly ordered and composed; they can unite only two wide, deep, individual worlds.—Young people—it is obvious—cannot achieve such a relationship, but they can, if they understand their life properly, grow up slowly to such happiness and prepare themselves for it. They must not forget, when they love, that they are beginners, bunglers of life, apprentices in love,—must *learn* love, and that (like *all* learning) wants peace, patience, and composure!

To take love seriously and to bear and to learn it like a task, this it is, Friedrich, that young people need.—Like so much else, people have also misunderstood the place of love in life, they have made it into play and pleasure because they thought that play and pleasure were more blissful than work; but there is nothing happier than work, and love, just because it is the extreme happiness, can be nothing else but work.—So whoever loves must try to act as if he had a great work; he must be much alone and go into himself and collect himself and hold fast to himself; he must work; he must become something!

For, Friedrich, believe me, the more one is, the richer is all that one experiences. And whoever wants to have a deep love in his life must collect and save for it and gather honey.

One must never despair if something is lost to one, a person or a joy or a happiness; everything comes back again more gloriously. What *must* fall away, falls away; what belongs to us remains with us, for everything proceeds according to laws that are greater than our insight and with which we are only apparently at variance. One must live in oneself and think of the *whole* of life, of all its millions of possibilities, expanses, and futures, in the face of which there is nothing past and lost.—

We think so much about you, dear Friedrich; our conviction is this: that in the confusion of events you would long ago, by yourself, have found your own solitary way out, which alone can help, were not the whole burden of your year of military service still lying upon you . . . I remember that after my locked-up military school period my craving for freedom and my distorted consciousness of self (that had to recover only gradually from the bendings and bruises that had been administered to it) would drive me into perplexities and desires that do not belong at all to my life, and it was my good fortune to have my work: in it I found myself and I am finding myself in it daily and am no longer looking for myself elsewhere. That is what we both do; that is Clara's life and mine. And you will also come to that, very certainly. Be of good courage, all is before you, and time passed in the difficult is never lost . . .

SAPPHO

Some Say that the Fairest Thing

Some say that the fairest thing upon the dark earth is a host of horsemen, and some say a host of foot soldiers, and others again a fleet of ships, but for me it is my beloved. And it is easy to make anyone understand this. When Helen saw the most beautiful of mortals, she chose for best that one, the destroyer of all the honour of Troy and thought not much of child or dear parent, but was led astray by Love, to bestow her heart far off, for woman is ever easy to lead astray when she thinks of no account what is near and dear. Even so, Anactória, you do not remember, it seems, when she is with you, one the gentle sound of whose footfall I would rather hear and the brightness of whose shining face I would rather see than all the chariots and mail-clad footmen of Lydia. I know that in this world man cannot have the best; yet to pray for a part of what was once shared is better than to forget it . . .

Permissions Acknowledgements

'To Friedrich Westhoff' by Rainer Maria Rilke reproduced by permission of W. W. & Norton Company on behalf of the Estate of Rainer Maria Rilke.

MACMILLAN COLLECTOR'S LIBRARY

Own the world's great works of literature in one beautiful collectible library

Designed and curated to appeal to book lovers everywhere, Macmillan Collector's Library editions are small enough to travel with you and striking enough to take pride of place on your bookshelf. These much-loved literary classics also make the perfect gift.

Beautifully made, every Macmillan Collector's Library book adheres to the same high production values. Each hardback features gilt edges, a ribbon marker and cloth binding, and every paperback has a bespoke illustrated cover.

Discover a new and exciting anthology or cherish your favourite classic stories with this elegant collection.

Macmillan Collector's Library: own, collect, and treasure

Discover the full range at
panmacmillan.com/mcl